John Clement

13 - 7 - 95

PAUL WATKINS MEDIEVAL STUDIES
The Early History of
The Abbey of Abingdon

PAUL WATKINS MEDIEVAL STUDIES
General Editor: Shaun Tyas
Consultant Editor: David Roffe
This new series is devoted largely to facsimile reprints of some of the great classics of medieval scholarship, but will also include some new studies.

---

1. ANDERSON, Alan Orr, *Early Sources of Scottish History, A.D. 500 to 1286*; a new edition with corrections, in two volumes (*forthcoming*).
2. HARMER, Florence E., *Anglo-Saxon Writs*; a new edition comprising the original work together with her later essay 'A Bromfield and a Coventry Writ of King Edward the Confessor' (1989).
3. STENTON, Sir Frank Merry, *The Early History of the Abbey of Abingdon*, reprinted for the first time since 1913 (1989).
4. FIELD, John, and SPITTAL, Jeffrey, *A Reader's Guide to British Place-Names* (*forthcoming*, 1989).
5. HILL, Sir Francis, *Medieval Lincoln*; reprinted with an introductory essay by Dr. Dorothy Owen (*forthcoming*, 1989).

The Early History of
The Abbey of Abingdon

By

Sir Frank Merry Stenton
(1880–1967)

PAUL WATKINS
STAMFORD
1989

Republished in 1989 by
Paul Watkins,
45, St. Leonard's Street,
Stamford, Lincolnshire, PE9 2HN,
with the permission of The British Academy,
20–21, Cornwall Terrace, London, NW1 4QP

ISBN 1 871615 07 0

Printed (on long-life paper) and bound by Woolnoughs of Irthlingborough

University College, Reading
Studies in Local History

The Early History of
The Abbey of Abingdon

By

F. M. Stenton, M.A.
Professor of Modern History, University College, Reading

Reading
Published by University College
1913

OXFORD: HORACE HART
PRINTER TO THE UNIVERSITY

NOTE

BY THE GENERAL EDITOR

WHEN in 1908 Mr. F. M. Stenton was appointed Research Fellow in Local History at University College, Reading, it was understood that one of the objects to which he would devote attention would be the elucidation of the early history of Abingdon and its abbey. The present volume, the second relating to Berkshire history produced by Mr. Stenton in this series, gives the results of his work. The cost of its publication has been defrayed by a grant made by the Council of University College.

The Research Fellowship in Local History, which had been rendered possible by the generous gifts of Mr. C. E. Keyser and Miss May, expired in July, 1912. But I am happy to say not only that it has proved possible to establish on a more permanent basis a Fellowship devoted in the first instance to archaeological study, but also that University College, Reading, is to continue to have the advantage of being able to claim Mr. Stenton as a member of its academic staff. For in July, 1912, he was elected to our Endowed Professorship of Modern History. No personal event in the history of the College has given me greater pleasure. Mr. Stenton was one of my first pupils at Reading: from Reading he proceeded to my old College at Oxford with an open scholarship; after his Oxford career and early publications had justified the hopes formed of him long before by those who knew him best, he returned at my invitation to Reading as Research Fellow; and now as Professor of Modern History in succession to myself he takes active charge of a subject and a responsibility to which for obvious reasons my own attention has for some years been little more than nominal.

If my own efforts in that field have produced results, I should look for it in the growth amongst us at Reading of a living interest in the study of local history as a means of illustrating the wider study of national history. I have handed over my responsibilities to my old pupil, colleague, and friend with all the more satisfaction because I know well that under his sympathetic and able guidance the future of our young school of local historical study is secure.

W. M. CHILDS.

PRINCIPAL's LODGE, READING,
January 6, 1913.

PREFACE

AMONG the secondary evidences which relate to early English history, the collected archives of religious houses claim an important place. In the present essay the documents relating to one of these early monasteries and the narratives of its foundation are examined with reference to their bearing upon the general history of England between the seventh and the tenth centuries. The Abingdon series of records is long, and, from the geographical position of the house, of peculiar importance for the period with which this essay deals. It is, for example, only Abingdon documents which demonstrate the annexation of Berkshire to the Mercian kingdom in the first half of the ninth century. The plan of the essay does not include a discussion of the documents and narrative which relate to the history of the abbey under the Anglo-Norman kings; but it is shown that this portion of the text, though only preserved in manuscripts of the thirteenth century, is the work of an author who ceased writing early in the reign of Henry II. It thus becomes contemporary evidence for the history of the Thames valley in the generation after 1100. To this generation, also, must be referred the earliest form of the foundation legend of Abingdon. It is suggested below that this legend, when allowance has been made for the invention of unhistorical detail, may fairly be allowed to illustrate the condition of southern England towards the close of the seventh century, and that an authentic outline of the early history of the house can be recovered from the materials which were compiled by its inmates in the Norman age.

F. M. STENTON.

UNIVERSITY COLLEGE, READING,
December 1912.

LIST OF ABBREVIATIONS

A. C. 'Historia Monasterii de Abingdon.' Edited by the Rev. Joseph Stevenson (Rolls Series). 1858.

Asser. 'Asser's Life of King Alfred.' Edited by W. H. Stevenson. 1904.

C. C. 'The Crawford Collection of Early Charters and Documents.' Edited by A. S. Napier and W. H. Stevenson. 1895.

C. D. 'Codex Diplomaticus aevi Saxonici.' Edited by J. M. Kemble. 1839–1848.

Chron. 'Two Saxon Chronicles parallel.' Edited by the Rev. Charles Plummer. 1892.

C. S. 'Cartularium Saxonicum.' Edited by W. de Gray Birch. 1885–1893.

D. B. 'Domesday Book.' (Record Commission.) London. 1783–1816.

D. B. and B. 'Domesday Book and Beyond.' By F. W. Maitland. 1897.

D. C. B. 'Dictionary of Christian Biography.'

E. H. R. 'The English Historical Review.'

Eyton. 'Court, Household, and Itinerary of King Henry II.' By the Rev. R. W. Eyton. 1878.

G. P. 'Gesta Pontificum.' By William of Malmesbury. Edited by Hamilton (Rolls Series).

H. E. 'Venerabilis Bedae Historia Ecclesiastica Gentis Anglorum.' Edited by the Rev. Charles Plummer. 1896.

Hist. Reg. 'Historia Regum.' By William of Malmesbury. Edited by the Rev. William Stubbs (Rolls Series).

Stubbs, Dunstan. 'Memorials of St. Dunstan.' Edited by the Rev. William Stubbs (Rolls Series).

THE EARLY HISTORY OF
THE ABBEY OF ABINGDON

I

THE writings which are printed under the common title *Chronicon Monasterii de Abingdon* were published under the direction of the Master of the Rolls in 1858.[1] They have thus been known to scholars for many years, and no authority has more frequently been cited as evidence for Old English and Anglo-Norman law and custom. The Abingdon series of land-books was employed in Nasse's classical work on the English village community,[2] and Freeman made large use of the later documents in the collection in his description of the Anglo-Norman settlement. The Abingdon evidence has always been considered of the highest value in relation to such subjects as these.

For the purposes of this essay it is necessary to distinguish between three manuscripts, all preserved in the British Museum, known respectively as Cott. Claudius C ix, Cott. Claudius B vi, and Cott. Vitellius A xiii. These texts are of very unequal value for the early history of the abbey. The third, written like the other two in a hand of the thirteenth century, and apparently for the use of the Abingdon cell of Colne in Essex,[3] is of the least authority in this matter. Its author was imaginative, and on the basis of the few facts preserved in the tradition of the house constructed a romantic narrative of its foundation

[1] Edited by the Rev. Joseph Stevenson. They form the second volume in the collection which is commonly known as the Rolls Series. The editing of these texts does not bear detailed criticism. In 1858 little work had been done upon Old English diplomatic, and it would not be expected that the editor's criticism of the land-books in the series should have value at the present time. It is more serious that he cannot be trusted implicitly to give the exact reading of his texts (e.g. Æthelbaldi for Æthilbaldi, below, p. 12). His identifications of sites mentioned in the course of the work are often wildly inaccurate and have misled many subsequent scholars. The whole plan of the edition, by which the latest MS. was adopted for the text, is faulty.

[2] *Zur Geschichte der mittelalterlichen Feldgemeinschaft in England.*

[3] This is rendered probable by the final paragraph, relating the works of Prior William of Colne (A. C. ii. 294–5).

to which undue credence has commonly been given. For the Abingdon texts strikingly illustrate the practice of mediaeval chroniclers to multiply fictitious detail. Many folios were devoted in the thirteenth century to events which a former age dismissed in a few phrases.[1] The importance of Cott. Vitellius A xiii mainly consists in its occasional record of facts which are omitted from the work of earlier writers. It is, for example, from this late authority that we obtain the important statement that the earliest religious community at Abingdon included only an abbot and twelve monks.[2] An occasional independence of judgement is shown by the writer of Vitellius A xiii; he will at times differ from his predecessors in his estimates of character.[3] But in general this independence is only displayed in relation to events of a later period than that which concerns us here.

MS. Claudius C ix is written in a hand of the early thirteenth century; Claudius B vi is always referred to a date some fifty years later. The relation between these texts has been accurately stated by their editor: Claudius B vi is 'a revised and improved copy' of Claudius C ix. In the early portions of the work,[4] with which this essay is chiefly concerned, the difference between the texts is most strongly marked. Claudius C ix opens with a paragraph describing the foundation of the abbey, and thereafter for many folios is restricted to a succession of charters connected by brief sentences of narrative. The writer of Claudius B vi was more ambitious. The opening folios of the manuscript have been mutilated; in its present state the work begins with a description of the conversion of King Lucius by Pope Eleutherius. There follows an account of the arrival in Britain of an Irish monk named Abbennus, who received from the British king a great part of Berkshire, in which he founded a monastery named Abbendonia upon a hill between two streams just beyond the vill of Sunningwell. Three hundred monks, and more, joined Abbennus there, and monastic life continued on the site until the arrival of the English in Britain. The text has just described the invitation extended by Vortigern for help against the Picts and Scots, when it is interrupted by

---

[1] This is well shown by a comparison of the foundation narrative given by Claud. C ix with that which opens Claud. B vi.

[2] A. C. ii. 272.

[3] As in the case of Abbot Ethelhelm (A. C. ii. 283-4).

[4] A. C. i. 1-13.

the loss of two folios ; and when the tale is resumed it is found
to have reached the time of Cædwalla of Wessex.

The baptism at Rome of this king is described, and his
epitaph is copied at length from Bede. The following clause
of the manuscript is headed *Descriptio villae Seuekesham postea
Abbendoniam appellatae.* It was clearly the belief of the writer
that the monastery was translated to this site in the time of
Cædwalla: relics were found there, and more particularly the
black cross *ex clavis Domini ex magna parte conflata et facta.*
In honour of the Holy Cross and St. Helen, a house of nuns was
founded at Helnestou by the Thames, and ruled by Cille, sister
of Hean, to whom the site of ' Sevekesham ' had been given by
Cædwalla. Until a great war between Offa king of the Mercians
and Kinewulf king of the West Saxons the nunnery continued
upon this site, but when a castle was built upon Wittenham hill
the nuns withdrew and the house came to an end. Meanwhile, the
monastery founded at ' Seuecesham ', the future Abingdon, continued under the government of Hean, its first abbot.

It is clear that this tale belongs to the region of romance :
nor have we reason for believing that its later phases are more
truly historical than is its opening. The house of nuns founded
by Cille belongs to the same order of ideas as the congregation
of three hundred monks which gathered round Abbennus at
Sunningwell. Some of the reasons which prompted the tale
are sufficiently plain. The writer of Claudius C ix knew that
the word *dun* in place-names normally denoted a hill [1] ; he knew
that the town of Abingdon does not stand upon a hill ; hence
the story of the foundation upon the heights by Sunningwell,
and the migration to the Thames. In the time of St. Æthelwold, when the foundations of the later abbey were being dug,
a black cross was found on a woman's body within a grave : [2]
charters known to the writer of the story showed that a lady
named Ceolswyth was associated in early gifts with the founder
of the monastery. We may believe that Cille was once current

---

[1] It is not certain that this was
always the case. There are other
examples of place-names compounded with *dūn* in which the
meaning of 'hill' is impossible—
for instance, Farndon, Nottingham-
shire, in flat land by the Trent.
In these cases 'dun' may mean
merely an expanse of open land
without reference to its height.

[2] Compare A. C. i. 7 with A. C. ii.
270.

as a short form of this name, and the tale of the early house of nuns was an easy invention on the basis of these facts. It clearly will not do to cite this story as representing incidents in the history of the seventh century.

It is necessary to emphasize the inferior authority of Claudius B vi upon matters relating to the foundation of Abingdon, because it is concealed by the way in which the history of this house has been edited. The printed text of the *Historia Monasterii de Abingdon* is conflate. As representing the expanded version of the narrative Claudius B vi has been taken as the text of the History, although numerous passages have been incorporated into the body of the work from Claudius C ix. The result is that Claudius B vi is made to appear as of equal authority with Claudius C ix. If the narrative which is presented in the latter manuscript had been composed at a date subsequent to 1200 this would not matter; between two thirteenth-century chronicles, fifty years apart, there is little difference in authority when their subject-matter relates to the age beyond the Conquest. But an examination of Claudius C ix shows conclusively that it is a copy of a work written by one who was an inmate of Abingdon monastery before the year 1117.

With regard to the date of this original narrative we are dependent entirely upon internal evidence. The anonymity of its author is absolute. He rarely vouches his personal knowledge of incidents as evidence, but he departs from his custom in one passage which serves to determine his date. He has described the good works of abbot Faritius, the restorer of the fortunes of the house after its sufferings in the last years of William II. He then remarks ' pallia serica amplius quam lx vidimus eum emisse et ad ecclesiastica ea ornamenta varios per usus distribuisse '.[1] On February 23, 1117, abbot Faritius died.[2]

Residence in the abbey at this time is also shown by the writer's comment on the events which followed the death of Faritius. ' Fuimus autem sine abbate iiii^or annis omnem tamen abundantiam victus et vestitus habentes. Praefuit vero huic domui quidam ex nostris venerabilis vir, nomine Warengarius qui a tempore Rainaldi abbatis prioris functus officio strenue nos gubernavit ac velut benignissima mater sinceriter semper

---

[1] A. C. ii. 48–9.   [2] Chron. *sub anno*.

fovit.'[1] Interpreted strictly, this passage would mean that the
writer was a member of the house of Abingdon already before
the death of abbot Rainald in 1097.[2] But it is in any case
clear that the author of this work died, or at least ceased
to write, before the close of the year 1170. On several occa-
sions he refers to Henry II by the phrase ' Henricus junior '.[3]
Such an expression, proper enough for a writer who had known
but one King Henry, would not have been employed of Henry II
after the coronation of his eldest son. And there is more definite
evidence than this. In the manuscript Claudius C ix, the hand
which has written the whole previous text of the History ceases
abruptly at the foot of folio 175 with the record of an agreement[4]
between abbot Walchelin [1158–64] and one Pagan of Appleford.
At the beginning of the *verso* of this folio another hand has
copied the great charter which Richard I issued in favour of
the abbey at Gisors on March 29, 1190. The conclusion
follows that the scribe who in the early thirteenth century
wrote the existing Claudius C ix was content to copy the text
before him without attempting any continuation. In Claudius
B vi such a continuation is made, and a succession of meagre
entries carries the history of the abbey down to the accession of
Richard I. But Claudius C ix is a simple transcript of a
manuscript written before 1170.

How long before it is difficult to say. But there is a distinct
probability that this work, composed, it will be remembered,
by a man already a monk before 1117, had reached its present
limits before the death of abbot Walchelin on October 31, 1164.
This event is not recorded ; and the phrases in which Walchelin's elevation to the abbacy is described, are such as might
fittingly be employed by a monk in relation to a living abbot.
' Cui (sc. Ingulfo) a rege in loco pastoris substituitur Walkelinus,
ecclesiae Eofeshamnensis monachus, vir circa possessiones ecclesiae sibi commissae fidelis et prudens, in revocandis quoque
priorum pastorum negligentia perditis studiosus.'[5] None of the
documents entered in Claudius C ix include any names which
point to a later date than 1164, and no reference is made in

---

[1] A.C. ii. 158–9.
[2] A.C. ii. 42.
[3] A.C. ii. 186, 210, 215.
[4] Attested by Adam of Catmere,

sheriff of Berkshire, who entered
upon his office at Christmas 1160.
[Eyton, 337].
[5] A.C. ii. 215.

the text to any event which need be placed later than this year.

It follows from these details that the portion of the Abingdon History which deals with events later than the death of abbot Faritius is the work of a contemporary author. For the local history of the Thames valley in the reigns of Henry I and Stephen the History becomes an authority of the very first rank. Between the local and general history of the twelfth century no hard line can be drawn. The incidents relating to the anarchy of Stephen's reign which are recorded in Claudius C ix are told by an eyewitness; the information contained in this text with respect to the early Norman age may be drawn at first hand from men who had known the rule of William I. It is only a reasonable belief that in Abingdon in 1117 there were old monks, inmates of the abbey under abbot Ealdred in 1066. There is no other record extant which gives on contemporary authority so detailed a picture of the life of any region of England in the twelfth century. For the student of the Anglo-Norman government it is well that the monks of Abingdon abandoned their national chronicle in 1066, and found a writer able to produce so full and accurate a record of the events with which his house was immediately concerned.

II

During the movement of monastic reform which resulted in the establishment of the Benedictine discipline in the churches of Wessex in King Edgar's reign, the fortunes of the abbey of Abingdon acquire an importance which belongs to them at no other period. The history that began when King Edmund gave the abbey of Glastonbury to Dunstan would have followed a very different course had not King Eadred granted the *monasteriolum* of Abingdon to Dunstan's follower, Ethelwold. It was at Abingdon that English monastic life was first affected by the example of the discipline which prevailed in the religious houses of Flanders and Burgundy. When Ethelwold sent his monk Osgar from Abingdon to learn the rule of the church of St. Benedict of Fleury he brought the house over which he ruled into touch with the strictest expression of the monastic life manifested in his day in Western Europe. It was from Abingdon rather than from Glastonbury that the new monasticism of the tenth century derived its distinctive features. The cathedral church of Winchester was colonized by monks from Abingdon; and at Winchester, in a synodal council summoned by King Edgar, the rule developed by Ethelwold at Abingdon[1] was formally promulgated for acceptance by the monasteries of the Benedictine order throughout England. It was under the guidance of Ethelwold's immediate disciples that the monastic life was introduced at Ely, Peterborough, and Thorney.[2]

Nevertheless, it must be admitted that utter obscurity overhangs the history of the abbey of Abingdon in the period which precedes the re-edification of the house by Ethelwold. We are, indeed, entitled to believe that an ancient monastery existed on the site occupied by the later abbey, but no consistent narrative can be written of its history. There have been preserved no contemporary references to the first monastery of Abingdon, such as are derived in the instances of Ely and Medeshamstede[3] from Bede, and in the instance of Glastonbury from the letters of St. Boniface. No consistent tradition was preserved in the house with regard to the succession of its abbots; its foundation legend is a pious, but incoherent, invention of the twelfth century. Once only does the name of Abingdon occur in a literary context which may be assumed to date from beyond the year 950[4]; and in this passage the existence of a monastery there is ignored. It is evident that there was no real continuity between the abbey of the eighth century and the house over which Ethelwold presided as abbot.

The earliest evidence which we possess with respect to this first phase in the history of the abbey dates from the reign of Ethelred II.[5] Between 1006 and 1009 Ælfric, abbot of Eynsham, a neighbour of the monks of Abingdon, and an admiring friend of St. Ethelwold, asserts that a little monastery had been maintained in Abingdon of old time, which, when Ethelwold received it, was poverty-stricken and deserted, with mean buildings and possessing but forty hides. The remaining

---

[1] The 'Regularis Concordia'. See C.S. 1138.
[2] We learn this on the authority of Ælfric of Eynsham (A.C. ii. 262).
[3] For Ely see H.E. iv. 19; for Medeshamstede, H.E. iv. 6.
[4] See below, pp. 44–5.
[5] A.C. ii. 257.

land which belonged to Abingdon, in what sense will be considered later, is asserted to be held by the king in right of his
office. In 993, in the course of a long and solemn charter of
which the original is still extant,[1] Ethelred II is made to say
that ' the estate which is called Abingdon ' had been given to
Our Lord and St. Mary by King Cædwalla. In the same
clause the king uses words expressing the belief that a certain
Hrethun, a prelate known from other sources to have lived in
the early ninth century, had ruled the house as abbot and
obtained for it various immunities from Pope Leo III and
Cœnwulf king of the Mercians.[2] These passages do not go
very far; but they are sufficient to prove the existence of
a monastery at Abingdon before the time of St. Ethelwold, they
point to an early tradition that the house had been founded in
the seventh century, and they thus give external support to
certain documents preserved in the abbey cartulary of which the
intrinsic authenticity is by no means apparent. It will, nevertheless, be well to remember that these texts, our earliest
evidence, are three hundred years later than the reputed foundation of the abbey, and also that more than another century was
to pass before William of Malmesbury, writing his *Gesta
Pontificum*, gave the first outline of what was to become the
accepted history of the beginning of the house.

When, towards the middle of the twelfth century,[3] an unknown
monk began the narrative which is the basis of the existing
Historia Monasterii de Abingdon, there lay before him but a
slender store of material from which information respecting the
foundation of the house might be derived. Slender as it was,
there is only too good reason for believing that much of this
material had itself been fabricated only a few years before it was
employed in the compilation of the History. The suspicion that
the compiler of the History had himself fabricated the documents
which he cited as evidence would be unworthy; his narrative is
too incoherent to have been thus founded. His work seems to

[1] Cott. Aug. ii. 39.

[2] As *presbiter abbas* he attests,
for example, the contemporary
C. S. 348, issued on November 25,
814. His profession of obedience
to Wulfred, archbishop of Canterbury, is printed as C.S. 355. It
is undated, but Hrethun attests
as bishop in 816 (C.S. 356, 357,
358).

[3] For the establishment of this
date see above, pp. 4–6.

represent an honest effort to frame a history out of materials too fragmentary for coherence.[1]

But this admission, which may fairly be made in relation to the nucleus of the printed History, must certainly not be extended to cover the whole of that composite work. Questions of date and authorship are of peculiar importance here. It has already been remarked [2] that the oldest copy of the History, the manuscript Claudius C ix, presents the work of a man who was a monk of Abingdon before the year 1117. His narrative did not satisfy his successors; they embellished his tale with additions for which no evidence has ever been quoted, and the inadequate editing of the published text of the History conceals the inferior authority of their work. If we rate at their proper value the imaginative exercises of thirteenth-century monks, any attempt which we may make to discover the circumstances under which the abbey came into being must turn on the evidence of the earliest manuscript, and on that alone.

It is to the credit of this early writer that he has little that is definite to say about the origin of the abbey. He can only tell us that he has received 'upon the authority of the ancients' that Cissa, 'king of the West Saxons,' gave a place for the worship of God to one 'Hean', an abbot, and to Cille his sister, and that Cædwalla, succeeding Cissa, added twenty hides at Abingdon to his gift. For the latter statement the historian vouches a fragment of a charter which is certainly spurious; it occurs later in the History among the boundaries of a forged charter of Eadred, and need no more be considered here. He then introduces the text of four documents which carry the history to the close of the reign of Ini, Cædwalla's successor. One of these documents, purporting to be the will of 'Hean', may summarily be dismissed; in every respect it is at variance with authentic Old English testaments. The remaining three documents deserve particular study. The first is a highly composite record. It begins, with a brief proem, by

---

[1] Most of the spurious documents in the Abingdon collection bear the known characteristics of Early Norman work. That they were not fabricated by the writer of the earliest text of the History for the purpose of his narrative seems clear from the fact that narrative and charters do not at all neatly fit in with each other.

[2] See above, pp. 4–6.

adopting the form of a charter of Cædwalla, stating that that king has rendered to abbot Hean 173 cassates near Abingdon, which King Cissa had granted to him and to Cille his sister.[1] The second sentence asserts by way of explanation that King Ini had taken possession of the land and 'restored it to the state' (reipublicae restituit), since no monastery had been built there, nor even an oratory. In the third sentence the charter form is resumed, and Ini monarc Saxoniæ is made to restore the land which Cissa and his other predecessors had granted to 'Hean the patrician' and Cille. The remainder of the document purports to be a statement by an unnamed abbot relating to the foundation of the abbey. Upon the restoration of the lands 'Hean' subjected them and himself to the service of God, choosing the unknown to build and rule a monastery near Abingdon, and himself taking the vow of a monk under his authority. But within five years from this time Hean sought the assistance of Ini for the recovery of his inheritance, and the unknown restored to them the land of the monasteries —the plural is employed—which had been founded. He also rendered at this time 20 cassates to the east of Thames, which Cuthred the under-king, Ethelred king of the Mercians, and Ini himself had given, and also 10 cassates 'across the ford of Beskesford' and 100 cassates in Bradfield, given together by Ini and Cœnred, where the unknown had built a monastery. Finally, in the presence of Bishop Hedde of Winchester (676–705), Aldhelm, abbot of Malmesbury (circa 675–705), a certain Wintra, et omni familia nostra in ecclesia, the unknown released Hean from his monastic vow. The document ends with a conventional anathema, bears the date 699, and is attested by kings Ini of Wessex, Ethelbald of Mercia, and ten other witnesses, whose names, in several cases, are certainly derived from a lost charter issued by the latter king.

Various attempts have been made to argue the authenticity of different parts of this extraordinary document.[2] Every such attempt breaks down as soon as the clauses of this record are compared with the few genuine instruments of the time which

[1] C. S. 29.

[2] For example, by the Rev. Joseph Stevenson in A. C. ii. 495–7. Compare also E. H. R. xx. 693, an article which is affected by the absence of sufficient allowance for the gradual invention of detail.

have survived. No king of the seventh century would style himself *monarc Saxonie*, speak of restoring land to the state, or convey in a single charter so considerable an estate as 173 hides. Alike in its Latin and in its subject-matter, the narrative of the unknown abbot is highly anachronistic if regarded as a composition of Ini's time. The incongruity of its style with that of authentic writings of the period [1] is so patent that it is hardly necessary to remark that the practice of dating charters by the year of the Incarnation did not obtain in England before it was introduced in the chronological writings of Bede, and that the formula of the dating clause *Scripta est vero haec cautionis singrapha*, permissible in a record of the tenth century, could not have been employed in a record of the seventh. [2] The motives which determined the fabrication of this document are not beyond recovery, but they will most fittingly be discussed after a brief review of the remaining three documents of the series.

The second charter runs in the name of King Ini, and grants to Hean, here styled abbot, 15 cassates in Bradfield, 15 at Bestlesford, 25 at Streatley, and 80 at ' Æaromundeslee'. It is of interest as including a very ancient conveyancing formula : the king, for the better security of his gift, places turves from the land at issue upon a book held by Beorht-weald the Archbishop of Canterbury and Daniel the Bishop of Winchester. Nevertheless the charter cannot be accepted as it stands. It bears the date 5 July, 687, and is witnessed by Ethelred king of the Mercians, who resigned his throne in 704, and by Daniel of Winchester, who received that see in 709. It contains the clause *Ego Winberctus hanc cartam scripsi et subscripsi*; and the writers of genuine charters do not attest them in England before the Conquest. It conveys to Hean a group of large estates, which would have been made the subject of separate grants in the seventh and early eighth

---

[1] The compiler of this record was acquainted with the Anglo-Norman general charter of confirmation, the continental *pancarte*.

[2] The Shaftesbury Cartulary includes a document bearing date 759, in which mention is made of a certain Wintra as formerly abbot of Tisbury in Wiltshire (C. S. 186). A Wintra abbas subscribes after Hæha the document, already cited, which proves Hæha's existence (C. S. 108). Probably all three references relate to the same person.

centuries. The facts which underlay its composition will be considered a little later.

The third charter of this series stands on a different plane. It is very brief, and a full text may be given here: 'Ego Ini rex Westsaxonum pro animae meae remedio redidi terram xlv cassatorum Hean patricio et Ceolswithae ad monasterium construendum. Quae terra appellatur in Bradanfelda et Bestlesforda et alia quae nominatur Shetlea cum omnibus ad se pertinentibus. Cui donationi testes affuerant Ebba, Æthilbald, et Eadfrith filius Iddi et cum jussione episcoporum Ceddae, Germani, Winfridi. Quam terram primus dederat Eadfrith filius Iddi super altare in ecclesia quae ibi constructa est pro anima ejus. Ego Theodorus servus Dei archiepiscopus consensi et subscripsi.' Like the previous grant, this charter is only preserved in the oldest copy of the History, the manuscript Claudius C ix.

Now it is quite possible that here at last we are given a fragment of a genuine charter of Ini. The names of the three bishops must be excised; they are inconsistent with each other. But for the rest, the fragment includes several features which suggest an early origin, and it does not resemble the ordinary work of a twelfth-century forger. It is short: its proem and anathema have been omitted; the latter has possibly been employed in the composition of the charter which precedes it in the manuscript. The style *Ini rex Westsaxonum* is correct; the phrases *pro animae meae remedio, ad monasterium construendum, cum omnibus ad se pertinentibus,* occur in genuine records of the time. The spelling Æthilbald would alone suggest that an early original lay before the scribe who wrote the present text; it is fortunate that he did not modernize the form of this name.[1] The title *patricius* applied to Hean, a style denoting the dignity of an under-king or ealdorman, is appropriate with reference to a West Saxon magnate contemporary with Ini, and had become obsolete by the ninth century. The name of the

---

[1] On the significance of the parallel form Athilhardi in C.S. 1331, reference should be made to the note in C. C. 38. In the 'Rolls Series' edition of the Abingdon History the name is spelled Æthel-bald; Æthilbald is given in C. S. 101, and this is the reading of the manuscript. The argument which may be derived from this form in favour of the authenticity of the charter is very strong.

co-grantee Ceolswyth is inexplicable if the document is a forgery. It is natural to assume that Ceolswyth is the full name, of which the Cille which occurs in the other charters is a pet form. But Ceolswyth is unique as a feminine personal name, and its invention for insertion in this document would be pointless. Unique also in an uncompounded form is the name of Iddi,[1] whose son Eadfrith founded a church on the estate. And a further argument towards the authenticity of the charter may well be derived from the fact that to none of the lands here conveyed did the church of Abingdon lay claim in later years. Bestlesford is granted in a spurious charter of King Alfred to Bishop Denewulf of Winchester[2]; in 1086[3] the manor of Basildon which represents this estate was held by the king as of the fee of earl Roger of Hereford. Bradfield in Æthelred's time was given by a certain Ælfric to a lady named Wynflæd[4]; in 1066 it belonged to a certain Horling, in 1086 to William the son of Ansculf.[5] Streatley does not appear in any other record earlier than Domesday Book, in which it is entered under the fief of Geoffrey de Mandeville.[6] There was no reason why in the twelfth century a charter should have been forged giving these lands to Abingdon; and even an Anglo-Norman monk did not engage wantonly in the fabrication of documents useless to his house.

If this document really preserves the text of a genuine charter of Ini it is of much more than local importance. Early West Saxon land-books are rare, and most of them are derived from cartularies of ill repute.[7] Egbert is the first West Saxon king of whom a diploma has survived in the original text.[8] The length of Ini's reign, his personal character, and his traditional reputation as a benefactor to monasteries, have resulted in the attribution to him of a number of land-books, but with the exception of the present charter none of these documents survive analysis. The unfortunate practice of omitting

---

[1] This name reappears in the compound æt Iddeshale (C. S. 416). The site is now known as Shiffnal, co. Salop. Cf. I. L., p. 660, Idsall al Shuffenhall, a late fifteenth-century reference.

[2] C. S. 565.

[3] D. B. fo. 57.

[4] C. D. 693.

[5] D. B. i. fo. 60 b.

[6] D. B. i. fo. 62.

[7] More particularly those of Winchester and Malmesbury.

[8] C.S. 396, a Kentish book. C.S. 225 is preserved in a pre-Norman copy.

witnesses, which the scribe of Claudius C ix has followed here
as in copying many later land-books, has deprived us of the
attestations of Ini's council; the names of Cedd,[1] Germanus,
and Wynfrith, and probably the name of Theodore, are an
unhappy addition for purposes of embellishment. But they do
not affect the probability, established on other grounds, that in
this document we possess, in an incomplete form, an authentic
charter of King Ini, coming from the closing years of the
seventh century or from the first decade of the eighth.

This conclusion is supported by the fact that if we assume
the present charter to rest on a genuine basis, we can explain
much that is otherwise unintelligible in the composite document
which stands at the head of the Abingdon series of records.
The compiler of the History began his labours by recording the
tradition of his house that its first endowment was a grant of
land by the West Saxon 'king' Cissa to the abbot Hean.
Cissa he assumed to precede Cædwalla, himself the predecessor of Ini. The existence, therefore, in the Abingdon
scriptorium of a charter which showed that Hean was not yet
an abbot after the beginning of Ini's reign contradicted the tradition; it had to be explained. His explanation was to invent
the story of Hean's delay in beginning the monastery and his
subsequent release from his monastic vow. To account for
Ini's re-donation of lands to Hean the writer held it necessary
to assume their previous confiscation; to explain Hean's appearance as *patricius* in Ini's reign it was argued that he had
abandoned the monastic life. And to a monk of the twelfth
century there was good reason for the introduction into the
story of the unnamed abbot. No monastic writer would
willingly allow the bishop to intervene in such a matter; the
time of the fabrication of the composite charter was a period in
which monasteries were acutely jealous of episcopal supervision.
Perhaps it is to the credit of the fabricator that he did not
give to the unknown a name and a local habitation.

It is not argued that this explanation accounts for all the
difficulties presented by this complex and incoherent story.

---

[1] In the manuscript the name Cedde is written in slightly smaller letters and fainter ink than the rest of the document, but the difference is hardly enough to suggest interpolation.

After eight hundred years it is not possible to recover the exact mental processes of a monk of Abingdon in the twelfth century. But to some such train of ideas the facts point, and it is probable that we could speak with more certainty if we possessed the full body of evidence on which the story was based. For there is some reason to believe that, in addition to Ini's second charter, other authentic records were employed in the work of fabrication, though they are no longer extant. Both the composite record and the first charter of Ini contain features which are hardly to be explained as pure invention. The forms Cœnred, Bradanfeltha, Æaromundeslee suggest that these names are derived from some source older than the twelfth century. The use of the formula 'Signum manus Ini —Ethelredi—Ethelfrith' marks early authentic texts.[1] The anathema of the composite record 'Si quis vero contra hoc decretum abbatatus venire temptaverit . . . sciat se coram Christo rationem in ultimo vivorum et mortuorum examine redditurum' has a number of early parallels. 'Si quis autem hanc donationem violare temptaverit sciat se in tremendo examine tyrannidis ac praesumptionis suae Deo rationem terribiliter redditurum' is the phrase in which Æthelbeald of Mercia ends a charter of which the original is still extant.[2] Correspondences of which this is given as an example can hardly result from chance, obvious as this reflection may be.

This last argument, it is true, is to some extent discounted by the fact that certain of these formulas reappear in documents, ostensibly of this period, which are even more obviously spurious than is the first charter of Ini. The forgers of documents of Ini's time, whether in the interests of Abingdon, Malmesbury, Winchester, or Westminster, seem to have made use of a common stock of formulas; and although it is probable that these are derived in the last resort from some authentic origin, their affiliation cannot be determined without a more searching inquiry than has yet been accorded to them.[3]

---

[1] C. C., p. 37.

[2] C. S. 154.

[3] The whole business of determining the genealogical relations of different cartulary texts requires detailed investigation. A religious house would go far afield for models upon which to fabricate its charters. Westminster Abbey, after the Conquest, obtained copies of ancient documents from the archives of St. Denis (C. C. 90, 92).

Their appearance in the Abingdon series cannot, upon the existing evidence, be entirely explained, but it may be suggested that the abbey of Malmesbury is the quarter to which suspicion points most definitely. The prominence given in the composite record to Aldhelm, the most famous abbot of Malmesbury, is suggestive; the attestation of Winbercht, who both wrote and subscribed the second charter, occurs also in spurious Malmesbury documents. To most of the formulas employed in this group of Abingdon documents parallels may be cited from the Malmesbury Register. And there remains the significant fact that Faritius, abbot of Abingdon in the early twelfth century, the very time when most spurious Old English land-books were produced, had been sacrist of Malmesbury and had made researches in the archives of that house when writing his life of St. Aldhelm. Provisionally, at least, we may fairly look to Malmesbury as the immediate source of the early formulas employed in the first charters of the Abingdon series.

This does not by any means rule out the possibility that authentic documents, which have disappeared, may lie behind these early Abingdon fabrications. There is no obstacle to the belief that Cuthred, a seventh-century regulus, may have combined in a grant of lands east of Thames to 'Hean' with Æthelred of Mercia. Ini may, as the composite record states, have been associated with his father Cœnred in the gift of the Bestlesford-Bradfield estate. These statements are possibilities; the only difficulty is that they occur in a document which, as it stands, is a flagrant twelfth-century forgery. But on one most important point the evidence of these charters may fairly be trusted: the name Hean appears to represent a real person who was living in the first decade of the eighth century. In a genuine list of witnesses appended to a forged document derived from the Malmesbury Register [1] there occurs the attestation of Hæha (v. l. Heaha) abbas; and the form Hean, which alone appears in Abingdon documents, merely represents an oblique case of this

---

[1] C. S. 108. On these attestations see Chadwick, *Studies on Anglo-Saxon Institutions*, p. 286. The document is a grant of liberties to West Saxon churches. Its formulas do not occur in undoubted texts of the eighth century, and the introduction of the Incarnation date 704 is a highly suspicious circumstance. But this does not affect the authenticity of the list of witnesses.

name, treated as a nominative by scribes to whom the declensions of Old English had become unfamiliar. The name is unique[1]; so that we need not hesitate to identify the abbot of the Malmesbury Register with the *patricius* of the Abingdon History, and as Hæha's attestation of the Malmesbury document must be placed in or before 709,[2] we must refer the origin of the monastery which he founded to some period previous to this year. And so again we obtain a confirmation of a seventh-century date for the beginning of the abbey of Abingdon.

Now the justification of this date is a matter of some interest apart from its bearing upon the foundation of the abbey of Abingdon; for it carries back the story to that enigmatical period of West Saxon history which lies between the death of Cenwalh in 672 and the rise to power of Cædwalla in 686.[3] 'When Coinwalch was dead,' says Bede, '. . . sub-reguli assumed the kingship of the nation, and held it divided among themselves for about ten years.' It is surely significant that the 'king' Cissa, to whom the first grant of lands to Hæha is assigned, is referred by the Abingdon tradition to just this decade of anarchy. If the name of Cissa and his donation of land to Hæha are inventions, they are singularly pointless. Cissa was not known to later ages as a founder of religious houses; unless he is the man denoted by the phrase *Signum manus Cisi*, which occurs in the attestations of two spurious seventh-century charters,[4] his name is only recorded in connexion with the foundation of Abingdon. His association with this event was accepted by William of Malmesbury when in 1125 he wrote his *Gesta Pontificum*. Abingdon monastery, according to this independent writer, was founded by Cissi, father of King Ini.[5] Beyond this vague tradition nothing was known about him at Malmesbury, nor was anything more definite preserved in the

[1] The name Hæaha is a weak formation from the stem Heah, frequently compounded in O.E. personal names, such as Heahmund and Heahbeorht. It is possible that the name Heaha, although it has never been identified, may exist in local nomenclature. Under such conditions the name would be indistinguishable from the O.E. adjective heah ='high'.

[2] When Aldhelm, bishop of Sherborne, an attesting party, died.
[3] H. E. iv. 12.
[4] C. S. 63, 71.
[5] G. P. 191. The opinion of Dr. Stubbs that Cissa was described as Ini's father to bring the monastery at Abingdon into connexion with Ini's house has much probability (D. C. B. *sub* Hean).

memory of the house, of which he was the reputed founder. In
the thirteenth century he was identified with the man who gave
his name to Chisenbury camp, the earthwork which overhangs
the Bath Road near the eastern border of Wiltshire; Bedwin,
it was then asserted, was the metropolis of his kingdom.[1] It
will not be disputed that the origin of this work lies many centuries behind the time of Cædwalla and Ini; but the fact that the
inventor of this identification found it necessary to travel fifty
miles before he could find a place with which the name of Cissa
could be brought into relation shows conclusively that his personality was not inferred from local nomenclature nearer home.
If once we believe it possible that the inmates of a religious house
in the twelfth century could remember the name of its founder
in the seventh, there is no reason for doubting that here again
the Abingdon tradition has preserved a trace of authentic fact,
and that in the traditional Cissa the true name is recorded of one
of the obscure sub-reguli whose rule in Wessex is attested by the
evidence of Bede.[2]

In view of the foregoing considerations it becomes possible at
last to indicate in bare outline the course of events which may
be assumed to have attended the foundation of the Abbey of
Abingdon. Towards the close of the seventh century Cissa, an
under-king in Wessex, made a grant of lands for the foundation
of a monastery to one Hæha, himself a man of noble birth. The
exact position of the lands then given cannot be determined, but
it may be surmised that they are represented in the large estate
at Æaromundeslee confirmed to Hæha in Ini's first charter.
The name of Æaromundeslee was giving place to the existing
name of Appleton in the tenth century, when the place was given
by King Eadmund to his *comes* Æthelstan,[3] and the modern
Appleton is only five miles from Abingdon. It is uncertain
whether a monastery was founded immediately upon the gift of
this estate by Cissa; Hæha himself undoubtedly continued
in the lay world, for he bore the title of *patricius* in the early
part of King Ini's reign. Before the century had closed Hæha

---

[1] A. C. ii. 268–9.

[2] Frithuweald, an under-king in
Surrey, contemporary with the
traditional Cissa, is only known as
the founder of Chertsey Abbey.

His name occurs, like that of Cissa,
in charters of ill repute, but there
is no reason for doubting his existence.

[3] C. S. 777.

had received a further grant of land from the latter king; lands situated twenty miles from Abingdon in the neighbourhood of Streatley and Bradfield. The accumulation by a single person of several estates designed for the foundation of monasteries is an attested feature of the social order of the seventh century. The practice was deprecated by Bede as dangerous to the well-being of the kingdom of Northumbria [1]; the example of Hæha may fairly entitle us to trace its operation in Wessex also. Finally, in or before 709, Hæha had entered the religious life and become an abbot, and the whole consensus of tradition is with us if we assume him to be ruling a monastery established at Abingdon. [2]

Whatever uncertainty in detail must attend any discussion of the origin of the abbey, it is at least clear that it was purely a West Saxon foundation, the reputed work of a noble of that kingdom, and associated with the name of one of its most famous rulers. It is therefore remarkable that a considerable number of the early documents put forward in later times as evidence for the tenure of lands and privileges should purport to have been issued by kings of the rival nation of the Mercians. It is irrelevant to remark that certain of these documents are flagrant forgeries; for a forged charter may well embody a genuine tradition, and among these early Mercian grants there is one, and that the most important of the series, which is undoubtedly authentic. We shall probably be near the truth if we associate the traces of Mercian overlordship preserved in the Abingdon History with the sporadic, but ultimately successful, attempts made by the greater kings of the Mercians to extend their territories to the valley of the middle Thames.

It is evident that at least as early as the year 635 a wide expanse of territory under the northern escarpment of the Chilterns formed part of the dominion of the king of Wessex. So much is proved by the establishment of the first bishop of the West Saxons at Dorchester on Thames, [3] but there remain facts

[1] Epistola ad Egbertum archi-episcopum.

[2] That a grant of land *ad mona-sterium construendum* did not of necessity mean the immediate foundation of a religious house there is shown by a comparison of two Worcester documents. By C.S.

154 Æthelbald king of Mercia gave to his *comes* Cynebeorht, for religious purposes, land at Ismere near the river Stour. In C.S. 220 Ceolfrith, Cynebeorht's son, de-scribes the land as *terram meam et hereditatem patris mei.*

[3] H. E. iii. 7.

which suggest with some force that the English occupation of this territory was accomplished independently of the formation of the original Wessex to the south of the river. The Cuthwulf who in 571 conquered from the Britons the land between Ayles-bury and Eynsham [1] may plausibly be identified with the Cutha whom the West Saxon genealogies assert to have been the brother of their king Ceawlin, but even so, the movement which Cuthwulf led was clearly distinct from the almost contemporary expansion of Wessex to the south and west under the leadership of Ceawlin and his son Cuthwine. With the accession of Cuth-wulf's son Ceolwulf to the chief kingship in Wessex, the lands north of Thames would naturally be added to the more ancient possessions of the West Saxon house, but it is highly probable that it was the memory of their independent conquest which, between 675 and 685, determined the creation of a second bishopric of Dorchester under the protection of Æthelred king of the Mercians.[2] In any case, the fact itself is evidence that the Mercian power had temporarily been extended to the Thames at the very time in which, according to tradition, the monastery of Abingdon came into being. It therefore shows a sense of historical congruity that the monks of Abingdon, when forging documents illustrative of the foundation of their house should have made Æthelred of Mercia a party to two of the charters which they composed at that time. We cannot, it is true, discover what basis of fact or fiction lies behind the introduction of Æthelred's name into these documents; but it is definitely possible that this king may have assisted in the creation of the monastery of Abingdon.

It is further probable that in the later seventh century Mercian influence was permanently dominant to the north of the upper Thames. The enigmatical people of the Hwiccas, a race possibly of West Saxon origin, which occupied the valley of the lower Severn, also included within its borders part at least of the modern county of Oxford. The name of Wychwood forest [3] is derived

---

[1] Chron. *sub anno*. This an-nexation is there described as the result of an English victory at *Bed-canford*, a site usually identified with the modern Bedford. To this identification there are very grave philological objections.

[2] H. E. iv. 23. The fact rests on the authority of Bede, and the text is clear. Needless doubt has been cast on this passage.

[3] Huiccewudu in C. S. 432.

from the name of this people, and in the thirteenth century Wychwood forest extended to Stowood and Shotover[1]; Hwiccian princes in the seventh century granted lands on the Cherwell for religious purposes.[2] Bishops of Worcester in the ninth century were still interested in estates on the middle Thames.[3] Whatever may be the date of that famous document which is known as the Tribal Hidage, it is surely significant that in all texts of this record the Hwiccas immediately precede the Chilternsætna. The conclusion cannot be avoided that already by the beginning of the ˙eighth century the Thames was the normal boundary between the kingdom of Wessex and the provinces which were subject to the king of the Mercians. Much of the obscure history of the following age turns upon the successive attempts of Mercian rulers to carry their boundaries farther to south and west, and with these attempts the monastery of Abingdon was very intimately concerned.

The later definition of Mercia as the region between the Thames and the Humber has tended to obscure the fact that the kings of Mercia in the century of their supremacy never admitted that the southern river was the permanent limit of their power. In the eighth century Berkshire was a border county. The successive phases of the struggle for the middle Thames were never set in order by any early writer; the outline of the story can only be pieced together from scattered references in histories and land-books, and it is from Abingdon documents that the essential evidence is derived. At the moment when the house of Abingdon was, according to tradition, founded there is good reason for believing that the left bank of the Thames was temporarily annexed to the kingdom of the Mercians. Under no other circumstances is it possible to account for the contemporary establishment of a Mercian bishopric at Dorchester on Thames. On the other hand, the brief duration of this see suggests with some force that the lands east of Thames were recovered for Wessex by King Ini soon after his accession in 688; a conclusion supported by the probability that between 704 and 709 the kingdoms of the West and East Saxons were conterminous.[4] All our authorities assign to

---

[1] Shown by later perambulations of the forest.
[2] C. S. 57.
[3] C. S. 509.
[4] Cf. C. S. 115.

Ini a long and prosperous reign; the resignation of Æthelred of Mercia in 704 was followed by the successive rule of two weak kings, and Wessex for the first quarter of the eighth century remained the most powerful among English kingdoms. It does not appear that the position of Wessex was immediately affected by the resignation of Ini in 726,[1] but when Bede in 731 finished the writing of his Ecclesiastical History Æthelbald of Mercia was the recognized overlord of all the English rulers whose provinces lay to the south of the Humber.

During his reign, which lasted from 715 until 757, there occurred the second extension of the Mercian kingdom to the valley of the middle Thames. A war between Wessex and Mercia in 738 was marked by the Mercian capture of a place named Sumortun, a site to be identified with the royal manor of Somerton in Somerset more probably than with the village of that name in Oxfordshire on the Cherwell.[2] From the evidence of Bede it is certain that the Mercian overlordship was generally admitted before this event, but there is no reason for the assumption that Somerset was the only field of the war of 733, and no other date so probably marks the re-establishment of Mercian power upon the Thames. With that re-establishment the monastery of Abingdon was nearly concerned, for it can be proved that Æthelbald exercised direct authority to the west of the river, in the county of Berkshire. An important document copied into the Register of Christ Church, Canterbury, relates that Æthelbald gave the monastery of Cookham, an institution otherwise unknown, to that house.[3] No record has been preserved of Æthelbald's dealings with the monastery of Abingdon, but it may well be significant that certain names of witnesses clearly derived from a lost charter of that king are incongruously annexed to one of the spurious documents invented in the twelfth century in the name of King Ini. If Æthelbald really made a grant of lands or privileges to Abingdon, and there is nothing unreasonable in the supposition, the circumstances of his grant would become unintelligible when the memory of his brief dominion in Berkshire had passed away, but the names of

[1] For this date see C.C., p. 39.
[2] The fabricated charter of King Æthelbald copied in A.C. i. 38–40 is no evidence.
[3] C.S. 291.

his Mercian companions could be employed in the Norman age to garnish a fabricated West Saxon charter without risk of detection.[1]

His murder in 757 was followed by a year of confusion. In the interval between Æthelbald's death and the establishment of Offa, the strongest of the Mercian kings, it is probable that the Thames valley once again passed within the kingdom of the West Saxons. It is at least certain that the royal estate of Bensington, on the left bank of the river, was in the hands of King Cynewulf of Wessex when the war of 779 broke out between him and Offa of Mercia. It has always been admitted that the capture of Bensington in this war marked the final annexation to Mercia of the debatable land east of Thames along the Chilterns. Documents preserved in the Abingdon History go far to demonstrate the further fact, ignored by more recent historians, that the battle of Bensington not only gave to the Mercian kingdom the whole line of the middle Thames for a boundary, but also carried the Mercian dominion once more across the river to include, as possibly in Æthelbald's time, the county of Berkshire.

The twelfth-century historian of Abingdon explicitly states that Offa defeated Cynewulf of Wessex in war, and added to his rule all the country between the Icknield Way from Wallingford to Ashbury on the south and the river Thames on the north.[2] The historian further asserts that Offa gave to the abbey the vill of Goosey in west Berkshire, and he records a general confirmation of title and a grant of privileges,[3] dated respectively in 811 and 821, both bearing the name of King Coenwulf of Mercia. These documents are undoubtedly spurious; the general charter of confirmation was unknown in England in the ninth century. But the evidence for Mercian rule in Berkshire rests upon surer foundations than these. The Abingdon

---

[1] Stranglic, for example, attests C. S. 137 and 157. Oba attests the same documents; he had been Æthelbald's companion in the days of his exile. Egfrid witnesses C. S. 181, the last charter issued by Æthelbald. Probably the Halda of the composite record stands for Ealda; a king's reeve of this name subscribes C. S. 191. An Aldberht signs both the composite record and the charter of Æthelbald given at C. S. 153, which is preserved in a late copy, but may be genuine.

[2] A. C. i. 14. Cf. Parker, *Early History of Oxford*.

[3] C. S. 352, 366.

History [1] contributes one charter to the short series of documents issued by Æthelflæd, Lady of the Mercians, King Alfred's
sister.[2] This charter cannot be accepted as genuine without
reservation; some one has tampered with its text and witnesses.[3]
But enough of the document remains without suspicion to
suggest interesting conclusions upon the political condition of
Berkshire in Offa's time. In form the charter is a grant by
Æthelflæd to one Eadric, her *minister*, of ten *manentes* at
Farnborough, which Eadric had bought from a certain Wulflaf,
to whose great-grandfather, named Bynna, the land had been
originally given by Offa of Mercia. It is not the general
custom of Anglo-Norman forgers to invent unnecessary genealogical details about imaginary persons, and the assertion about
the relationship between Wulflaf and Bynna is very probably
true. For it can hardly be a coincidence that a certain Bynna
is known to have been an ealdorman under Offa, and to have
attested his charters. As his attestation does not occur in any
documents to which Abingdon monks are known to have had
access in the twelfth century, it would be rash to assume that
his name was invented in the compilation of the Farnborough
land-book.[4] In any case, the tradition that north Berkshire
had in Offa's time been subject to the king of the Mercians
was undoubtedly strong in Abingdon in the Norman period.

Regarded alone, however, this evidence merely represents
the isolated testimony of a single, and then obscure, religious
house. It is immensely reinforced by an incidental statement
in that Canterbury document,[5] already quoted, which proves the
Berkshire dominion of Æthelbald of Mercia. Offa, according
to this record, 'took away the monastery of Cookham and very
many other towns (*urbes*) from King Cynewulf, and added them
to the Mercian *imperium*.' The Register of Christ Church is
written in a hand of the late thirteenth century, and its compiler

[1] A. C. i. 44–6.

[2] C. S. 632–3.

[3] The charter is dated 'die v idus
Septembris in loco qui dicitur
Weardburg.' The Mercian Register
records under 915 that Æthelflæd
built a *burh* at Weardbyrig, and
the Mercian Register is entered in
the Abingdon text of the O. E.

Chronicle. The first witness after
Æthelflæd is 'Ælfwyn Episcopus.'
Ælfwyn(n) is a feminine name,
borne, as the same chronicle relates, by Æthelflæd's daughter.

[4] C. S. 187, 207, 256, 274. Most
of these attestations come from
Worcester.

[5] C. S. 291.

has treated the documents before him with considerable freedom. Internal evidence suggests the authenticity of the present record, and as no connexion can be established between Abingdon and Canterbury documents, the statement regarding Offa's appropriation of Cookham has all the force of independent testimony. In one respect, indeed, it contradicts the Abingdon tradition. Cookham is in the extreme east of Berkshire, far below the line of the Icknield Way, which at Abingdon was regarded as forming the southern limit of Offa's annexations. There is thus reason for believing that the whole of Berkshire, and not merely the northern third of the shire, was annexed to the Mercian kingdom at this time. A contradiction of this kind serves to emphasize the independence of the Abingdon and Canterbury traditions.

More significant information is derived from an Abingdon document, hitherto unnoticed, of which the authenticity is above dispute.[1] In 844, Ceolred, bishop of Leicester, gave to King Beorhtwulf of Mercia fourteen hides of land at Pangbourne (*æt Pægeingaburnan*) 'to secure the freedom of certain monasteries'. This transaction does not stand alone; eight years previously bishop Heahbeorht of Worcester, by a similar grant, had obtained immunities for Hanbury monastery from Beorhtwulf's predecessor, Wiglaf. The interest of the Pangbourne charter[2] is twofold. As the document was preserved among the Abingdon muniments, the house there was undoubtedly interested in the privileges which it conveyed. Abingdon was one of the monasteries which then obtained this 'freedom'; and the existence of a monastic community at Abingdon in 844 is thus placed beyond doubt. Equally certain is the evidence of the Pangbourne charter that Berkshire remained subject to the Mercian kings until within six years of the middle of the ninth century. Had this document been a simple grant of land it might, though with difficulty, have been explained away. But there can be no question that the king who grants immunities to a religious house within a shire is for the time being the accepted lord of that shire.

Another feature of the Pangbourne charter now becomes suggestive. Immediately upon receiving the land at Pangbourne,

[1] C. S. 443.   [2] C. S. 416 (original).

E

Beorhtwulf proceeded to re-convey it to his ealdorman Æthelwulf. It is reasonable to suppose that the privileges conferred by the charter upon the local monasteries diminished the revenue which the ealdorman derived from the region under his charge. In the Worcestershire case of Hanbury, to which reference has already been made, it was necessary for the bishop to make gifts of land to two ealdormen. But the appearance of an ealdorman named Æthelwulf ruling Berkshire in 844 under the Mercian king brings the Pangbourne charter into relation with general affairs at a very critical moment of the national history.[1] The name is common, but the Berkshire Æthelwulf can be identified as a witness to a Berkshire charter of Æthelswyth, wife of Burgred of Mercia in 868, and he was commanding the local forces when the Danes invaded his shire in 871.

In him, therefore, we must recognize a Mercian ealdorman set over Berkshire, who at some undefined date transferred his allegiance to the king of Wessex. It is very probable that the course of events which began the military operations of 871 in Berkshire was affected by the ealdorman's possession of an estate at Pangbourne. Three days after the establishment of the Danish army at Reading in that year, a raiding party under two jarls met and defeated Æthelwulf at Englefield.[2] It can scarcely be coincidence that the place of battle lay three miles from Pangbourne, by an ancient road running south from that village.[3] It looks as if Æthelwulf, with the men of his house-

[1] Two contemporaries of this name must be distinguished from the Berkshire Æthelwulf : (1) a *dux* who attests Kentish books from 838 to 873 ; (2) an Æthelwulf who witnesses Worcester charters for Mercian kings from 836 to 866. In 884 another Æthelwulf appears as witness to west Midland charters (C. S. 552). He is probably the brother of Ealhswyth, King Alfred's wife, who died in 903. He was the son of an ealdorman Æthelred who bore the second name Mucel, under which he is a frequent signatory of Mercian documents. That his province was occupied by the enigmatical people named the Gaini we know from Asser. An earlier Mucel, pre-

sumably his father, attests many Mercian charters, most of which relate to Worcestershire. As no contemporary of this name is known, the elder Mucel may fairly be identified with the Mucel Esning who as ealdorman received land at Crowle in Worcestershire when Hanbury monastery obtained its liberties from King Wiglaf. This is a strong argument for placing the Gaini in the east of Worcestershire.

[2] Chron. *sub anno* 871.

[3] This road probably forms part of the line, of which the continuity is now lost, which connected Silchester with Dorchester on Thames.

hold and lands, had used this road to intercept the invaders, raiding westward from Reading. Four days later the ealdorman perished in the course of King Æthelred's unsuccessful attack on the Danish base. His Mercian origin supplies a convincing explanation of the remarkable statement made by the historian Æthelweard to the effect that his body was taken for burial to the town of ' Northweorthige, in the tongue of the Danes, Derby'. No reason has yet been assigned for the burial of a Berkshire ealdorman in so remote a part of England. In this matter, as in others, Æthelweard's narrative gains credit from the discovery of new facts, for the truth can only be that Æthelwulf was carried back into his own country, in the heart of the Mercian kingdom. In 871 Burgred, the successor of Æthelwulf's former master Beorhtwulf, was still ruling the Mercians.

It would therefore seem to be proved that for more than sixty years after the battle of Bensington Berkshire remained a Mercian ealdormanry, subject, as Bishop Ceolred's dealings with King Beorhtwulf show, to the spiritual rule of the bishops of Leicester. In the eighth century the jurisdiction of bishops was still determined by the boundaries of kingdoms. This fact has an immediate bearing upon the tradition which, as early as the tenth century, associated Ceolred's predecessor Hræthun with the history of the monastery of Abingdon.[1] As developed in the twelfth century, the Abingdon story ran to the effect that ' Rethun ' had been a bishop in Mercia in the time of King Offa, and that, compelled thereto by the attacks of his enemies, he had resigned his see and retired to Abingdon, of which monastery he ultimately became abbot.[2] This tale is at once contradicted by an examination of contemporary charters, which show that Hræthun was abbot of an unnamed house from 814 until his elevation to the see of Leicester between 834 and 836. These dates tell heavily against the belief which was current at Abingdon in the tenth century that Hræthun, as abbot, obtained privileges for his house from Pope Leo III.[3] It is true that Archbishop Æthelbeard of Canterbury, under authority of this pope in 803, secured privileges for all the churches of

[1] C. D. iii. 264. See above, p. 8.   [2] A. C. i. 15.
[3] C. S. 312.

his province. Many abbots set their crosses to the archbishop's decree, but the name of Hræthun does not appear among them. A confused memory of this event is sufficient to account for the Abingdon tradition; and the fact that already in 993 those interested in the history of Abingdon were in error upon a point of this kind serves to emphasize the discontinuity of monastic life there. But in view of the temporary incorporation of Berkshire at this time in the diocese of Leicester, the election to that see of an abbot of Abingdon would be a most appropriate event. Unless or until Hræthun's name is discovered in definite connexion with another religious house we may provisionally assign him to Abingdon.

These sixty years of Mercian rule in Berkshire are of considerable significance in relation to the general history of the time. In particular, the Mercian retention of this county suggests that the permanent importance of the victory won by Ecgbeorht of Wessex over Beornwulf of Mercia *æt Ellandune* in 825 has very materially been exaggerated. It may, perhaps, have facilitated the establishment of West Saxon supremacy over Mercia which was accomplished four years afterwards; it certainly did not avail to restore the integrity of the West Saxon kingdom south of the Thames. As to the circumstances which at last brought about the restoration of Berkshire to the kings of Wessex it is impossible to speak with certainty. The birth of the future King Alfred at the royal vill of Wantage in 849 suggests with much force that the transference had been accomplished before this date. On the other hand, the meagre entries in the Chronicle between 844, the date of Beorhtwulf's Pangbourne charter, and 849 make no mention of any event which is sufficient to occasion so considerable a change. Nor may we ignore the possibility that although a Mercian ealdorman continued in charge of the shire, the kings of Wessex retained their ancient estates within its borders. There remains what is perhaps the more probable argument that the final recovery of Berkshire was connected with the recorded negotiations of the year 853 between Mercia and Wessex. In that year Burhred king of the Mercians requested the help of Æthelwulf of Wessex against the north Welsh, and received Æthelwulf's daughter Æthelswyth in marriage. In 856 Æthelwulf is found granting land at Ashbury in Berkshire to one of his thegns,[1] and it is permissible to suggest that the cession of Berkshire may have been the price of Æthelwulf's assistance to Burhred, three years previously. The evidence is not sufficient to provide an accurate answer to this question, but from 860 onwards there is no doubt as to the position of the county. In that year Ealdorman Æthelwulf was associated with Osric of Hampshire in checking the Danish army which had just stormed Winchester.[2] In a different form Mercian influence was present in Berkshire after this date, for in 868 Æthelswyth, Æthelwulf's daughter and Burhred's queen, granted to her thegn Cuthred an estate at Lockinge which ultimately came into the possession of the monastery of Abingdon.[3] But such a fact as this does not affect the West Saxon government of the shire, and when in 871 the Danish army first took winter quarters south of the Thames, resistance was made by the men of Wessex, commanded by their rulers.

It would not be expected that during these seventy years of Mercian power in Berkshire the church of Abingdon would receive many gifts from West Saxon kings. It is therefore remarkable that the only two land-books now extant issued under the name of King Beorhtric of Wessex are derived from the Abingdon collection. The first of them[4] purports to be a grant by that king to his 'prince' Lulla of land at ' Eastun ', now known as Crux Easton in Hampshire; its formulas betray that it is a forgery, and it should not be cited as evidence for the ninth century. The second charter cannot be dismissed so easily. It records the gift by King Beorhtric to a prince named Hemele of land at Hurstbourne in Hampshire in exchange for another estate by the river Meon. It is unfortunate that the king is made to remark ' hanc donationem meam propriis litterarum caracteribus roboravi et singrafa Crucis confirmavi '. These phrases are not found in authentic instruments of Beorhtric's reign. With the exception of this single lapse, the document commits no anachronism, the names of its witnesses are almost certainly authentic, and the charter may reasonably be accepted as a genuine land-book of King

[1] C. S. 491.
[3] C. S. 522.

Chron. sub anno.
[4] C. S. 282.

Beorhtric, incongruously modified in a single phrase by the writer of the Abingdon History.

But this gift of Hurstbourne opens up a wider question. Among the fraudulent charters in the *Codex Wintoniensis* which bear the name of Edward the Elder there occurs a passage which asserts that Ecgbeorht, the king's great-grand-father, acquired from the community at Abingdon fifty *manentes* at Hurstbourne and gave in return an equal territory at Marcham in Berkshire.[1] That this story was known at Abingdon is proved by the insertion into the History of a charter by which Ecgbeorht is made to give 'that monastery Marcham' as fifty *manentes* to Abingdon in 835.[2] A Berkshire grant by Ecgbeorht in that year would, if genuine, seriously affect the arguments which suggest the Mercian government of this region through-out the time of Ecgbeorht's rule in Wessex. Internal evidence is strong enough to condemn the charter; its compiler, not content with asserting Ecgbeorht's gift of Marcham, has in-serted a short custumal into the document reciting the privileges which he conceived to belong to his church, and has shown in so doing that he wrote at a time when the outlines of Old English law were becoming confused.[3] No clerk in the ninth century would have composed the phrase 'pretium . . . sanguinis peregrinorum, id est Weregeld'. The man who wrote these words was acquainted with the Norman *murdrum*. Not until the reign of Edgar did the church of Abingdon obtain posses-sion of Marcham. With the condemnation of Ecgbeorht's Marcham charter there disappears the only land-book which implies West Saxon rule in Berkshire between 779 and 854.

There can be no doubt that Abingdon was among the religious houses which perished in the course of the Danish invasion of Wessex in the year 871. If the monastery escaped the first attack of the army moving from Thetford to its new base at Read-ing, it lay in the path of one of the raids which compelled the West Saxons to make peace with the invaders at the close of

---

[1] C. S. 592.

[2] A. C. i. 33. C. S. 413.

[3] These passages rank in point of date with the *Leges Henrici Primi*. The references to the 'angyld' in C. S. 366, and the present charter, occurring as they do in fabrica-tions of the Norman age, are in-teresting illustrations of early Anglo-Norman law. Cf. D. B. and B. 290-2.

the year. The tradition of the house was clear as to its over-
throw. The Danes drove the monks into flight and destroyed
the monastery so that nothing except the walls remained. It
was, however, remarked that the relics and charters which
belonged to the house were secretly preserved; a fact which
bears definitely upon the authenticity of the earliest Abingdon
documents.[1] Before long the ruined monastery appears to have
been re-inhabited; but its continuous life had been broken, and
the first phase in its history ends at this point.

In describing the events which immediately followed the
disaster of 871, the Abingdon historian introduces the name
of King Alfred in a manner which is of considerable general
interest. 'After the death of King Æthelred', he says, 'his
brother Ælfred assumed power. He alienated the vill in which
the monastery is placed, . . . with all its appurtenances from the
said monastery, rendering to the victorious Lord an unequal
return for the victory with which he was endowed.'[2] The
writer of the second text of the Abingdon History expands
these sentences, remarking that Alfred added evil to evil, and
comparing him to Judas among the twelve apostles. Such
passages are in marked contrast with the general tenor of
opinion about King Alfred, and they have naturally attracted
attention.[3]

It is obvious that King Alfred does not deserve this violent
reprobation. On any disinterested view, there is little wrong in
the confiscation of the estates of a derelict monastery. But the
exact nature of Alfred's action is less than clear. It is certain
that in Æthelstan's time, and later, when Abbot Ethelwold
undertook the charge of the monastery, the vill of Abingdon
was in the king's hand.[4] It is less certain whether, before the
Danish war, the house of Abingdon had ever been other than
a little monastery built upon the royal demesne. There is no

---

[1] A.C. i. 47. 'Reliquiae sanc-
torum, cum cartis ipsius domus,
quas superius in hoc libro annota-
vimus, et inferius sunt annotatae
clandestine sunt reservatae.'

[2] A.C. i. 50.

[3] E. G. Plummer, *Two Saxon
Chronicles*, ii. 113. The author
has not examined the story from

the Abingdon side.

[4] The decayed monastery of Ely,
when bought from Eadgar by
Abbot Æthelwold, was in the
king's hand. A.C. ii. 262, 'Erat
tunc destitutus et regali fisco dedi-
tus.' The parallel with Abingdon
is close.

adequate evidence that the monastery had ever possessed the whole of the lands which belonged to Abingdon. Here, again, it is well to remember how small a body were the monks of Abingdon in the first two centuries of their house. The one relevant statement which suggests unlawful action on Alfred's part occurs in King Æthelred's great charter of 993. After describing the restoration of the house by Kings Eadred, Eadwig, and Eadgar, Æthelred is made to remark, ' For the aforesaid kings, restoring to the church of God the estate (*rus*) which is called Abingdon, . . . in which our predecessors, deceived with devilish avarice, had unjustly built a royal building for themselves, forbade that any king should require entertainment (*pastum*) there or raise a building at any time.' Against this definite charge of wrong must be placed the silence of Abbot Ælfric, who, without any hint of recent usurpation, merely remarks that the hundred hides which belonged to Abingdon were held by the king *jure regali*. At the close of the tenth century an exact memory of the local position in Alfred's day could hardly be expected : the monks of Abingdon were interested in giving the sanction of ancient possession to their tenure of the whole vill of Abingdon. The question cannot be wholly answered; and there remains a doubt of which the benefit may fairly be given to King Alfred.

It is uncertain how long the life of the monastery was interrupted. Of one estate which remained with the abbey until the Dissolution the title was derived from a charter of King Alfred. The five-hide village of Appleford on the Thames, some three miles below Abingdon, was sold by that king for fifty mancusses of gold to his faithful Deormod.[1] The document which records the sale is one of the few charters of Alfred preserved in an authentic form : the absence of all churchmen from among its witnesses agrees well with the general ecclesiastical condition of Alfred's reign, and the king is accorded the style Rex Anglo-Saxonum current at the close of the ninth century.[2] From Deormod or his heirs the estate passed to the Abbey of Abingdon and is entered among the estates of the house in Domesday.

The Abingdon History also supplies a charter to the brief

[1] C. S. 581.   [2] Upon this style see *Asser*, 149–50.

series of documents issued under the name of Edward the Elder.[1]
The charter relates to what is now the hamlet of Hardwell in the
parish of Woolstone, and is in form the grant of a new land-book
to a certain Tata the son of Æthelhun, the king's vassal, in place
of a similar document originally granted by King Æthelwulf,
but accidentally lost.[2] The church of Abingdon was not immediately concerned in this transaction; and Edward's charter[3] is
only entered in the Abingdon History because the Hardwell estate
ultimately passed to the abbey under the will of Eadwine, ealdorman of Sussex, who died in 982.[4] Eadwine, whose death is
entered in the Abingdon text of the Old English Chronicle,[5] was
buried in the abbey church there; but the obscurity which
attends the history of the noble families of the tenth century
conceals the nature of his connexion with Tata the son of
Æthelhun and the circumstances of his interest in Berkshire.
But the appearance of a South Saxon noble as a benefactor
to Abingdon may give warning against exaggerating the sepa-
rateness of the provincial divisions of England in Æthelred's
time.

Under these conditions Edward's Hardwell charter is no
evidence that a monastery was in being at Abingdon in his
reign.[6] The fortunes of the abbey become clearer with the
accession of Æthelstan. In a document of the year 930, the
name of an abbot, a certain Cynath, is at last recorded.
The document in question, by which Æthelstan is made to
give Dumbleton in Gloucestershire to the church of Abingdon,
is spurious in its present form, but the name of Cynath was also
preserved in the tradition of the house. He is described as
'Guiatus, who under Athelstan recovered all things which the
Danes, the companions of Inguar and Ubbar took away', in the

---

[1] C. S. 601.

[2] C. S. 600 is also the grant of a
new land-book by Edward in place
of a lost document issued by Æthelwulf. This may rouse suspicion,
but the close of the ninth century
was a time at which land-books
were likely to be lost. C. S. 600
comes from the thirteenth-century
Wilton Cartulary, which is not
known to be related in any way to
the Abingdon History.

[3] This document is rich in references to the open-field system, and
has often been cited on this account.
It is therefore peculiarly unfortunate that Kemble and Birch
should have identified the site with
Hordle in Hampshire. This mis-
take is corrected in V. C. H. Hants.

[4] A. C. i. 429.

[5] Ed. Plummer, i. sub anno.

[6] C. S. 667.

Chronicle Roll of the Abbots of Abingdon which has recently been printed.[1] The name Cynath, which represents a late contraction of an unrecorded O.E. Cynenoth, appears in two other land-books, one the Farnborough charter of Æthelflæd of Mercia, the other an early grant by Æthelstan preserved in the Hengwrt MS.[2] It is not certain whether the same person is denoted by each of these attestations, for the Chronicle of Evesham records an Abbot Cynath contemporary with Æthelstan. The existence of an abbot of this name in the year 929 is proved by the appearance of a ' Kenod abbas ' among the names of those who in that year were admitted to fraternity with the monks of St. Gall. The evidence, on the whole, seems sufficient to justify the insertion of Cynath in the list of the abbots of Abingdon.

In any case, the church of Abingdon in the early years of Æthelstan's reign was an institution capable of receiving gifts of land. This much is proved by a very remarkable document, preserved in both texts of the Abingdon History, by which Æthelstan the ealdorman granted the ' town ' of Uffington to St. Mary's Church. The document falls into three parts : first, a Latin notification of the gift ; then a long description of the boundaries of the estate, set forth in Old English after the manner customary in charters; and finally, a second notification, in Old English, corresponding to the Latin opening of the record. Documents of this kind are very rare ; in some ways the Uffington example is unique, and its Old English conclusion deserves translation :—' Æthelstan the ealdorman booked this land of Uffington into St. Mary's Church (stow) in the day of King Æthelstan, and that was done in the witness of Wynsige bishop of Berkshire and Archbishop Wulfhelm and Bishop Rodward and many others both bishops and abbots and thegns who were gathered there, where this town by these boundaries was added to St. Mary's property at Abingdon. And the Archbishop Wulfhelm and all the bishops and abbots that were summoned there excommunicated from Christ and from all Christ's community whoever should undo this gift or

---

[1] E. H. R. xxvii. 727–38.
[2] C. S. 642, ' Cynaht abbas.' For Cynath, from Cynenoth, compare

Ednath, from Eadnoth in the place-name Ednaston, co. Derby; thirteenth century, Ethnadeston (I. L. p. 251).

diminish this land in meadow or in boundary; be he sent away and thrust into hell bottom, ever without end. And all the people who stood around there said, "Be it so. Amen, Amen!"[1]

The grantor of this estate was Æthelstan, ealdorman of East Anglia, known later, from his great power, as the Half King.[2] He attained fame in later life as a benefactor and patron of monks, but his name is chiefly associated with the monasteries of the eastern counties, and it is only from the present document that we learn of his connexion with Berkshire.[3] His grant of Uffington is another proof that the estates of ealdormen in the tenth century were not confined to the districts over which they exercised official rule. The tenth-century ealdorman of East Anglia was lord of Uffington in Berkshire, just as the Norman earl of Chester was lord of Drayton and Buscot in the same county. Legally, the ealdorman's action in booking an estate to a religious house is of some interest. There is no reason for believing that he had received the estate from the king with any implied reservation to religious uses. No such royal charter was preserved among the Abingdon muniments. We may fairly accept the conclusion that in Æthelstan's reign a great noble already had the power of alienating his estates, in his lifetime, upon obtaining his heir's consent; and if he could alienate to a religious house, he could also alienate to friends or dependents. How far a lord could dispose of his own powers of justice or tribute-taking is a question to which no adequate answer can at present be given.

It is evident that the record of this grant which remained at Abingdon was composed after the event. The exact date of the gift cannot be determined, for the chronology of the early years of Æthelstan's reign is in such confusion that the names of the attesting parties are an insufficient clue. The gift was made in Æthelstan's reign, but the date of Æthelstan's accession has not yet been finally determined.[4] The year in which Wulfhelm

---

[1] C. S. 687.

[2] He first attests charters in 923. For Æthelstan see C. C. 82, 84.

[3] He received Wrington in Somerset from King Æthelstan, gave it to Glastonbury, and at last became a monk there.

[4] It is not possible to argue this matter at length here. The difficulty is caused by the fact that whereas the regnal years given in charters imply Æthelstan's accession in 924, the extant lists of O.E. kings assign him a reign of fourteen years, which, reckoned from his death in 940, mean that he

became Archbishop of Canterbury is unknown ; Wynsige, bishop
of Berkshire,[1] was one of the shire-bishops who appear from time
to time in this period, but nothing more is known about him.
The name of Bishop Rodward is of more assistance, for this
prelate may fairly be identified with the Hrothweard who in 928
attests charters as Archbishop of York.[2] As there is no record
of his translation to York from any other see, it would appear
that at the time of the Uffington grant, although consecrated
archbishop, he had not yet received the pallium and was not
therefore accorded the archiepiscopal title. If this opinion is
correct, the Uffington grant may reasonably be assigned to
927 or the beginning of 928.

The assembly in which the gift was made known in some
ways bore an anomalous character. It was not a shire moot :
the Archbishops of Canterbury and York are not likely members
of a Berkshire local assembly. That it was not a meeting of the
Witan may be inferred from the omission of any reference to the
king's presence. It was evidently a large gathering : the assent
of the 'people who stood around' is one of the more interesting
features of the record. It may be compared with another
assembly, later in the same century, in which also the church
of Abingdon was interested. For the sake of comparison, the
record in O.E. of this assembly, which is only found in the first
text of the Abingdon History, may be translated here[3] :

   ' Ælfheah the ealdorman bequeathed to Ælfhere the ealdorman
twenty hides at Kingston ; then Abbot Osgar requested Ælfhere
the ealdorman that he might obtain that land from him with

began to reign in 926. (See Stubbs's
Dunstan, lxxiv.) As Æthelweard
places Æthelstan's accession in 926,
and the Annals of St. Neots assign
to Edward the Elder a reign of
twenty-six years from his coronation in 900, I would suggest that
Edward died in 926, but that
Æthelstan had already been associated with him as joint king in
924.
   [1] The Latin version of the grant
reads 'kynsii'. Stubbs (*Dunstan*,
lxxxviii.) identified him with Cyne-
sige, bishop of Lichfield from 949,
and suggested that at the time of the
Uffington charter he might have

been administering Berkshire for
Odo, bishop of Ramsbury. But the
reading 'Wynsige' in the O.E. text
suggests a blunder in the Latin
version, and there is no difficulty
in the belief that a shire-bishop of
that name should only appear once
in the documents of the time. A
contemporary Wynsige was bishop
of Dorchester.
   [2] He followed an Archbishop
Æthelbeald, the exact date of whose
death is uncertain. Wulfstan,
Hrothweard's successor, became
archbishop in 931.
   [3] A.C. i. 335.

money; then the ealdorman agreed with him. And the abbot gave him then a hundred mancusses of gold.[1] Then after Easter there was a *micel gemot* at Athelwarabirig and it was told to the lords that were there, that was Bishop Athelwold and Bishop Ælfstan and Abbot Æthelgar and Eadwine and Ælfric Cild and Ælfric Siraf's son and Brihtric his brother and very many other thegns. And this was done with great witness, and the ealdorman Ælfhere took the counterpart of this writing as evidence.'

Ælfheah, ealdorman of Hampshire, died in 971; Æthelgar, abbot of the New Minster, Winchester, became Bishop of Selsey in 980; at some point in these nine years the present gemot was held. Here again we are dealing with no ordinary shire-moot: Æthelwold was the famous Bishop of Winchester, Ælfstan was Bishop of Ramsbury, Ælfhere was ealdorman of Mercia, the place of meeting lay within Wiltshire, and Osgar, Abbot of Abingdon, was present.[2] A copy of the will of Ælfheah was preserved in the cathedral monastery at Winchester; Ælfhere, the ealdorman's brother, received lands at Albourne in Wiltshire and Faringdon in Berkshire. Faringdon is known from later evidence to have been an estate with widely scattered dependencies, among which it is probable that the twenty hides at Kingston (Bagpuize) were included. The *micel gemot* of Æthelwarabirig,[3] attended by lords from at least three shires, may be compared with similar meetings recorded in documents of the Norman period; such as the plea in which the Bishop of Worcester proved his right to Alveston in Warwickshire before Queen Matilda *in presentia quatuor vicecomitatuum.*[4] The notification of an ealdorman's will, disposing of property in many shires, would naturally give occasion for the holding of a special assembly of this kind.

[1] The mancus expressed in gold the value of thirty silver pennies. The present passage is an important part of the evidence which suggests a gold currency in England in the tenth century.

[2] C. S. 1174.

[3] The name is of interest as a local compound of the feminine personal name Æthelwaru. The name, apparently, has not persisted in local nomenclature, but the place of meeting can approximately be identified from a passage in C. S. 1286, a Wilton document. The boundaries of land at Avon, co. Wilts., included a reference *to thæm wege the scæt fram Æambres buruh to Ethelware byrig oth hit cymeth to tham wege the scæt eastan fram winter burnan west to billan cumbe.* Evidently, therefore, Æthelware- burh lay near to Amesbury.

[4] D. B. i. fo. 238 b.

The gift of Uffington by Æthelstan the ealdorman was made directly to the church of Abingdon. The Abingdon History contains entries of charters in the name of King Æthelstan granting other estates immediately to the monastery, such as Shellingford on the Ock, Dry Sandford and Swinford in Hormer hundred, Dumbleton in Gloucestershire. None of these four charters can be accepted without qualification as authentic records of Æthelstan's time. There are, however, certain features in the Shellingford grant which suggest that the compiler of the History had before him some earlier record of the gift.[1] The king is made to convey twelve *cassati* in Shellingford to the church : Shellingford had been assessed at 12 hides in 1086, but its assessment had been reduced by William I to $2\frac{1}{4}$ hides. In the body of the charter the place-name appears in the form Scaringaford ; an earlier form, Scæringaford, is given by the writer of the first text of the History, which will account for the later renderings of the name and is not likely to have been invented in the twelfth century. It is more remarkable that the grant purports to have been made at the request of Godescalc the priest. Godescalc is unique as a personal name in England before the Conquest; the only bearer of such a name who enters into Anglo-Saxon history is the Wendish Prince Godescalc, who as a fugitive entered the service of Cnut. The name is of German origin; as borne by a priest at Abingdon in the year 931 it can best be explained with reference to those continental relations of King Æthelstan which are most clearly expressed in the marriages of the king's sisters. It is very possible that Æthelstan may have invited a continental scholar to take charge of a religious house upon a royal estate : the fact that Godescalc is styled priest rather than abbot agrees with our knowledge of the decay of monastic life at Abingdon at this time. At Abingdon in Æthelstan's reign there was a church, perhaps a school, but there was no monastery as the word was understood later in the tenth century. In any case, we may not assume that the personality of Godescalc the priest was an invention of the reign of Henry I.

Other estates which in the Norman period belonged to Abingdon were held in virtue of charters recorded under the

---

[1] C. S. 683.

name of King Æthelstan. In all cases, however, with the
exceptions which have already been noted, the king granted the
lands in the first instance to one of his thegns, and the church
only obtained the estates from the grantor or his heirs. Estates
obtained in this way were Watchfield, where Æthelstan granted
twenty *cassati* to his thegn Ælfric[1]; Farnborough, where the
king gave ten manentes to one Ælfheah; and Chalgrave in
south Bedfordshire, where Æthelstan confirmed to a certain
Ealdred lands which he had bought from the Danes in the reign
and by the order of Edward the Elder.[2] Early in the reign of
Æthelred II, a matron named Ælfgifu gave Chalgrave to
Abingdon, together with an unidentified estate called Bultheswurth which had been granted to a certain Wulfnoth by
Æthelstan in 931.[3] Before the Norman Conquest Chalgrave
and 'Bultheswurth' had passed from the possession of the
abbey. In 939, Æthelstan gave to the religious woman Eadlufu
fifteen *mansæ* at Brightwaltham; the charter is entered in the
Abingdon History, but there is no evidence that the monastery
ever occupied the estate.[4]

There is, indeed, evidence to the contrary. In 1086, Brightwaltham was held by Battle Abbey, exempt from payment of geld;
in 1066 it had belonged to Earl Harold, with an assessment of ten
hides; an unnamed thegn, Harold's predecessor in the manor, had
paid geld on fifteen hides,[5] which clearly represent the fifteen
mansæ conveyed by Æthelstan's charter. There is thus a strong
presumption that the charter is authentic, and the presumption
is confirmed by an examination of its witnesses. In the same
year 939[6] Æthelstan gave to another woman of religious con-
versation, named Wulfswyth, fifteen *mansæ* at Overton on the
Kennet in Wiltshire. The original text of the Overton charter
has been preserved; and is attested by nine bishops, four
ealdormen, and nineteen thegns. All the bishops and ealdormen, and seventeen of the thegns, attest the Brightwaltham
charter also. In outline, though with differences of verbiage,
the formulas employed in the two charters correspond, but
the correspondence ceases in regard to one essential matter,

[1] C. S. 682.
[2] C. S. 659.
[3] A. C. i. 428.
[4] On this charter, which is certainly authentic, see *Oxford Studies
in Social and Legal History*, ii. 74.
[5] D. B. i. fo. 59 b.
[6] C. S. 734.

the style accorded to the king in the *verba dispositiva*. In the Overton charter, Æthelstan is styled *divina mihi adridente gratia rex Anglorum et aeque totius Bryttanniae curagulus*; in the Brightwaltham charter he grants with the title *nodante Dei gratia basileos Anglorum et aeque totius Brittaniae orbis gubernator*. The difference is important; for the Brightwaltham charter is the earliest diploma of probable authenticity which assigns an imperial style to a king of England.[1] If the charter is genuine, as is suggested both by its structural details and by the absence of any motive for its fabrication, it is evidence that Æthelstan, in the last year of his reign, allowed himself to bear an imperial title. There is no reason for the assumption that the copyist of the Abingdon History wantonly changed some simpler phrase into *Dei gratia basileos Anglorum*; King Eadmund is styled *divina favente gratia basyleos Anglorum* in an original charter of the year 940.[2] The most reasonable conclusion would appear to be that one of the scribes of Æthelstan's court, inventing many varieties of royal title, at last lighted upon the phrase *basileos Anglorum*. As a royal style, the phrase agreed well with the inflated language employed in texts of the period; with the frequent substitution of Imperator for Basileos the imperial phraseology persisted in English diplomata until the eleventh century. In contrast to the opinion put forward by Professor Freeman, it may be inferred that Æthelstan's assertion of imperial rank was induced by no political considerations. It was the work of some chancery scribe, feeling his way towards some well-sounding form of words in which he might express his master's royal name.

It is highly probable that the 'religious woman' Eadlufu, on whom Æthelstan bestowed Brightwaltham, was a member of some monastic body. There is no such probability in the case of other persons to whom the Abingdon History assigns grants of land from tenth-century kings. It is a very noteworthy fact that a considerable number of the tenth-century land-books preserved in the Abingdon collection relate to estates in which the house of Abingdon had no known interest in later times. In

---

[1] Upon the question of the imperial styles assigned to English kings in the tenth century refer-ence must be made to C. C. 111.
[2] C. S. 748.

952 King Eadred granted to his vassal Ælfwine three cassati in Barkham. Three hides in Barkham are duly recorded in Domesday, but they belonged to the king in 1086, and had formerly been held by one Elmer of St. Eadward. King Eadwig in 956 gave five cassati in Padworth to Eadric his man. Padworth in 1066 was assessed at eight hides, but none of them belonged to Abingdon. Alestan held two hides and a half of King Edward; the rest of the village belonged in parage to three thegns. Eadgar in 966 granted Linslade in west Buckinghamshire to his relative, the matron Ælfgifu; his charter is recorded in the Abingdon History, but the estate, to our knowledge, never was held by the abbey. Earlier than this, in 944, King Eadmund had sold for ninety mancusses of most pure gold eight *mansæ* in Brimpton to his thegn Ordulf. There is no question of the authenticity of the charter in which the royal grant was made; in 1066 Brimpton had borne an assessment of eight hides, of which four hides and a half were held of King Edward by Beorhtric, three hides and a half by Godwine. By the date of Domesday, Beorhtric's land, now rated at three and a half hides, had passed to the Norman, Robert son of Gerold, Godwine's land, reduced in assessment to two and a half hides, was held of the fee of Ralf de Mortimer. Abingdon had no interest in the village; but no Abingdon forger in the twelfth century would have inserted its true pre-Conquest assessment in a fabricated land-book.[1]

So far as we can tell, none of these four manors ever came into the possession of the church of Abingdon. Various other charters in the Abingdon series also relate to properties outside the later demesne of the abbey. Compton near Ashbury, and Curridge, which Eadred gave respectively to his thegns Ælfheah and Ælfric; Stowe in west Northamptonshire, which Eadwig bestowed on his kinsman Bishop Brihthelm, were never lands of Abingdon. In other cases it is possible to show that the lands conveyed in extant land-books came into the possession of the

---

[1] In the early thirteenth century monks of Abingdon were acquainted with the description in Domesday of the estates of their house. In the original hand of Cott. Claud. C ix a copy of this portion of the Survey is set forth. But this by no means implies that in the previous century a charter could have been forged upon the basis of scattered entries elsewhere in the Berkshire Domesday.

church at a time considerably later than the date of the original grant. Winkfield was given by King Eadmund to the religious woman Sæthryth in 942 ; not until the reign of Æthelred II did Abingdon receive the estate from the noble woman Eadflæd.[1] But the most remarkable illustration of the secular character of the tenth-century land-book is afforded by the estates of the thegn Wulfric.

Between 940 and 958 a man of this name received seven charters from the successive kings of the period. By Eadmund he was granted fifteen *mansæ* at Garford; by Eadred, ten hides at Stanmore, five *mansæ* at Denchworth and twenty-five at Chieveley; by Eadwig, ten *mansæ* at Boxford and five at Charlton. In addition to these Berkshire lands, Wulfric received from Eadred, in a charter of which the original text is extant, eighteen *mansæ* at Welford in exchange for another estate in Cornwall, ' which the rustics of that district call by the barbarous name Pendyfig '.[2] Between 958 and 960 Wulfric committed some offence and his lands were confiscated; in the latter year he made peace with King Eadgar and received from him a charter of restitution. This document, of which also the original has been preserved,[3] restores to Wulfric Ashbury, Denchworth, Garford, Chieveley, Stanmore, Chaddleworth, Boxford, Benham in Berkshire; Tichbourne in Hampshire; Worthing, Stedham, Tillington, Patching, Poyning, and Nytimber in Sussex. Nothing is known of Wulfric's earlier possession of Chaddleworth; his tenure of Ashbury and Benham raises a difficult question through the facts that in 953 Eadred had given Ashbury to one Ælfsige and Eadgifu his wife, in 956 Eadwig had given Benham to Ælfsige alone. It cannot be decided whether purchase, descent, or exchange had brought these lands to Wulfric before the confiscation of his estates. But it is at least certain that there was no ecclesiastical reservation in the charters which gave him Garford or Stanmore or Chieveley. And the extent of his property has a more strictly historical interest as an illustration of the character of a thegn's holding in Eadgar's reign. Wulfric in 960 possessed lands in Berkshire, Hampshire, and Sussex; formerly, he had held in Cornwall also. Already in the middle of the tenth century the

[1] A. C. i. 429.   [2] A. C. i. 145.   [3] C. S. 1055.

properties of an English landowner were assuming the character
which belonged to them on the eve of the Norman Conquest;
they were collections of scattered manors.   Garford is eighty
miles from Worthing.

Most fortunately it has happened that we are able to answer
the question how the church of Abingdon came to possess the
title-deeds of manors in which the abbey held no territorial
interest.   In 1327 there was a riotous dispute between the
citizens of Abingdon and the abbey; a remarkable anticipation
of the greater storm which burst upon other monasteries in the
time of the Peasants' Revolt.   Charters were burned; and not
only the charters of the abbey, but those which other persons
had placed there for safe keeping in the past.[1]   In the destruction of 1327 we have beyond doubt the reason why so few
original texts relating to the abbey have come down to the
present time.   But the practice, incidentally revealed, of land-
owners laying up their charters for secure custody in the
archives of a neighbouring monastery has a very definite bearing
upon both the compilation of monastic cartularies and the nature
of the Old English land-book.   A great majority of extant land-
books are derived from cartulary texts; but it is never safe
without external evidence to assume that the estates conveyed
by a charter thus preserved ever belonged to the religious house
whose inmates have copied the document.   It will not do to
base the history of a great monastic territory, such as that of
Abingdon abbey, exclusively upon the records preserved among
its muniments.   And in view of the Abingdon evidence it is
legitimate to suggest that the land-book as the instrument of a
grant was in much more frequent use than is sometimes allowed.
Exceptional circumstances only have preserved the text of an
Old English diploma to the present time; the title-deeds of
a tenth-century family were exposed to risks of the gravest sort.
We may be certain that the extant land-books which refer to
secular estates form but a fraction of the body of charters issued
to the thegns of the tenth century.   In his classical essay upon
the Old English immunity the late Professor Maitland,[2] arguing
that powers of jurisdiction were implied in the liberties granted

---

[1] See the narrative of this rising in E. H. R. xxvii. 727–38.
[2] D. B. and B. 289.

by the normal diploma, argued also that the number of such diplomata was never vastly in excess of the collection which is before us to-day. 'We should have no warrant for the supposition that royal diplomata have perished by the hundred and left no trace behind'; such was his inference from the fact that the greater part of the Codex Diplomaticus is derived from the cartularies of a small group of religious houses. The analysis of these cartularies, the study of the subsequent history of the lands with which they deal, a work hardly begun as yet, will perhaps lead to a modification of this argument. It may lead to the conclusion that among surviving diplomata a considerable proportion were at the time of their compilation mere grants of land to secular persons, incorporated among ecclesiastical muniments either through the subsequent acquisition by the religious of the estates which they conveyed, or because of their deposit for safe custody in the archives of some monastery. Such conditions were very definitely exceptional, and the fact may suggest that the influence of the land-book as a means of secular endowment has commonly been under-estimated. Among the forces creating the private jurisdictions which existed in 1066 due weight is now given to the influence of personal rank and to the creation of jurisdictional dependence from the fact of dependent tenure. The Abingdon evidence suggests that the direct influence of the land-book in creating an immunity had a wider influence than is commonly assigned to it; an influence not confined to the great ecclesiastical estates among whose muniments most of the solemn charters now before us have been preserved. The justification of this suggestion must wait upon the further study of the great monastic cartularies of the south.

Of the royal charters executed in the reigns of Æthelstan and Eadmund and preserved in the Abingdon History few can have taken immediate effect as grants to that house. When Æthelwold received the abbey from King Eadred the monastic property consisted of only forty hides, and Abingdon itself was a royal estate. As such, it was the place where King Æthelstan received in 926 the ambassadors who in that year came from Hugh, duke of the Franks, to negotiate his marriage with Eadhild, Æthelstan's sister. The meeting gave occasion for a session of the Witan; the messengers gave many gifts to the king, some of which were bestowed by him upon various monasteries. Malmesbury received a portion of the Cross and the crown of thorns.[1] The witanagemot of Abingdon is recorded only by William of Malmesbury in a passage derived from a contemporary panegyric of Æthelstan which is now lost; it is the earliest reference to Abingdon thus far known. Apart from the texts and traditions of the abbey, its authenticity is confirmed by the absence of any suggestion that a monastery existed at that time in the place. It was not in any abbey, but in that royal building which the next generation assigned to King Alfred, that Hugh's representatives put forward their request.

Throughout the reign of Eadmund there is no direct evidence of monastic life at Abingdon. The house in later centuries possessed nine charters issued in the name of this king : all of them in detail are drawn up on the conventional lines and employ the stereotyped formulas followed in the royal scriptorium of the reign, and all of them may well be genuine. Comment has already been made upon some of the documents in this series. Among the remainder, the most interesting, from its context, is a charter relating to Culham on the Oxfordshire bank of the Thames, an estate which still belonged to the abbey at its dissolution. This village, as fifteen *mansæ*, was given by Eadmund to a matron of royal descent named Eadhild.[2] So far we are dealing with an ordinary grant of land, but a paragraph following the charter introduces a complication. It has been noted that King Æthelstan in 931 gave Watchfield to his thegn Ælfric. The compiler of the Abingdon History, after transcribing the Culham charter, states that Ælfric gave Watchfield to the church of Abingdon and that Eadmund made his confirmation of the gift conditional upon the lease of Culham by Godescalc the abbot to Eadhild. The latter was thenceforward to hold the estate as King Coenwulf[3] granted it to his sisters, who gave it to the house of Abingdon, to which the property was to return upon Eadhild's death. This explicit statement, which cannot easily be reconciled with the language of

[1] Hist. Reg. § 135.
[2] C. S. 759 (only recorded by Claud. C ix).
[3] Coenwulf was the son of one Cuthbeorht, and had two brothers, Ceolwulf I, who succeeded him in Mercia for two years, and Cuthred king of Kent.

Eadmund's charter, suggests that the writers of the Abingdon
History did not copy all the materials which lay before them at
the date of their work. It is improbable that in the twelfth
century any tradition was maintained of the circumstances
under which Culham first passed to the monastery early in the
ninth century. Unless the statement is pure invention, some
record of a gift by Cœnwulf of Mercia to his sisters must have
been kept in the abbey. The story cannot be tested further;
no sisters of King Cœnwulf are otherwise recorded, and the
absence both of any basis for the tale and of any motive for its
invention raises a presumption in favour of its truth. It would
add greatly to the interest of the incident if it were possible, in
Eadhild, the matron of royal race, to recognize a descendant
from the line of the Mercian kings.

With one exception, the remaining charters of Eadmund in
the Abingdon collection require no detailed comment. The
exception is a grant by Eadmund to a bishop named Ælfric
of one hundred *mansæ* at Blewbury. The grantee may safely
be identified with Ælfric I, bishop of Ramsbury in Eadmund's
reign; Abingdon at no time possessed any interest in the
property, and as a forgery the charter is meaningless. The
document is of interest as a re-grant made necessary by
the loss of an earlier charter; in the absence of the original its
authenticity is not above question. Genuine or spurious, it
belongs to a small but remarkable group of charters in which
a hundred hides are given as appurtenant to some estate.[1] In
a charter of Edward the Elder one hundred *cassati* at Micheldever were granted to the New Minster at Winchester.[2] By
a forged document preserved among the records of the cathedral monastery in that city, King Alfred is made to give one
hundred *manentes* in Cholsey to Bishop Denewulf. The boundaries set forth in Eadmund's grant of Blewbury touch the borders
of the villages of Brightwell, Hagbourne, and Cholsey; it is
a reasonable inference that the scribe who compiled the document believed that he was recording a gift of Blewbury hundred
as it existed in the tenth century. Neither the Micheldever,
the Cholsey, nor the Blewbury charter can be regarded as first-
rate evidence; all three documents are derived from cartulary

[1] C. S. 596.   [2] C. S. 565.

texts which cannot be controlled by reference to the originals. But we have no warrant for a definite denial that substantially they may be telling the truth about the local organization of the period to which they refer. Many facts combine to indicate that in the tenth century local divisions, regarded each as one hundred hides, were being annexed to royal estates. In 1086 Berkshire was divided into twenty-two territorial hundreds; of these, eleven were called by the name of some royal manor within their borders, and Blewbury was one of the eleven examples. The practice suggests a tendency towards centralization in the local government of the period; the king's bailiff in a royal manor was beginning to receive the profits of the local court, and to account for them among the revenues derived from the estate of which he was placed in charge. Oxfordshire and Shropshire are two shires, widely separated, in which this practice is known to have prevailed in 1066. If the Blewbury charter rests upon a genuine basis, it permits the argument that some system of the kind was already in operation in the year 944.[1] When all proper reservations have been made, the balance of probability is in favour of the authenticity of the Blewbury grant.[2] For we may revert to the question of motive, and safely argue that no monk of Abingdon in the twelfth century was at all likely to forge a lengthy document in favour of the Bishop of Salisbury, the successor of Ælfric of Ramsbury.

At this point we may return to the famous passage in which Ælfric of Eynsham describes the condition of the monastery of Abingdon in the reign of King Eadred. The *monasteriolum* possessed forty hides, the remaining land of the place, that is one hundred hides, was held by the king *jure regali*. The conclusion is very reasonable that in those hundred hides we should recognize the later hundred of Hormer, the northern corner of the county of Berkshire, annexed to the king's estate in Abingdon.

---

[1] On the subject of local divisions annexed to royal estates reference may be made to Chadwick, *Studies on Anglo-Saxon Institutions*, pp. 249–62.

[2] Bray, Reading, Blewbury, 'Nachededorn,' Bucklebury, Thatcham, Kintbury, Lambourne, Wantage, Shrivenham, Sutton. Marcham, which gave name to a hundred, was granted to Abingdon as 50 cassati by Eadgar. Probably before this it had been a royal manor at which hundredal dues were paid. The remaining Berkshire hundreds take their names from what appear to be ancient meeting-places.

In 1066 the hundred bore an assessment of 110 hides; we shall not seek an exact correspondence between the fiscal burdens laid upon a district in the mid-tenth and mid-eleventh centuries. But in one respect the statement of Ælfric is remarkably supported by the evidence of the charters preserved in the Abingdon History. In 1068 the whole of Hormer hundred belonged to the church of Abingdon; but almost without exception the several villages of the district came into the possession of the house later than the death of King Eadred.[1] Shippon, for example, rated at five hides, though claimed by the abbey as a pre-Conquest possession (A. C. ii. 19), seems to have been given to the monastery by Earl Hugh of Chester. Wootton, as ten *cassati*, was granted by Æthelred II in 985 to his thegn Leofwine. Cumnor, with its members of Hinksey, Seacourt, Wytham, and Eaton, was given to the church by Eadgar in 968 in a charter of which the extant text is not above suspicion. Kennington was given by Eadwig in 956 to the priest Byrhthelm, who afterwards exchanged the estate with abbot Æthelwold for lands in Devonshire. Bayworth and Sunningwell were members of Abingdon, and Abingdon we know to have been in the king's hand at this time. Only Swinford and Dry Sandford remain; charters of Æthelstan conferring these estates upon the church were put forward in the twelfth century, but they cannot safely be accepted as authentic. Not until the reign of Edward the Confessor was the hundred court of Hormer conferred upon the abbot of Abingdon. For those forty hides which the church possessed in 954 we must look beyond the limits of Hormer hundred.[2]

On the other side there must be set the definite statement of Ælfric of Eynsham that King Eadred gave to Æthelwold 'the royal possession which he had in Abingdon, that is, one hundred *cassati*'. There is no need to question Ælfric's authority upon a point of this kind, and such a grant would be a very natural endowment under the circumstances of the time. But in the tenth century there was no absolute certainty that the recipient

[1] Compare Hugh's charter, A. C. ii. 20, with D. B. i. fo. 58.

[2] It is very remarkable that Uffington, the one estate which we know to have been conferred directly upon the abbey before this time, bore in 1066 an assessment of exactly forty hides. There is a strong probability that this is the explanation of Ælfric's statement.

of a royal gift would enjoy the permanent possession of the land conveyed. Obscure as are the court politics of Wessex in this period, it is at least clear that Eadred's death was followed by a brief phase in which the land was ruled by men in little sympathy with the ideas of ecclesiastical reform which had influenced Eadred, and were to influence Eadgar more effectively. If, on Ælfric's authority, we accept Eadred's grant of the hundred hides appurtenant to Abingdon, the evidence of later charters will compel us to assume that the grant, if it ever took effect, was repudiated during the reign of Eadwig. The words used by Ælfric definitely imply that the restoration of monastic life at Abingdon was suspended during this time. ' Non coepit tamen abbas designatum sibi opus in diebus Eadredi regis, quia cito obiit, sed regnante Eadgaro honorabile templum . . . construxit.'[1] If the building of the church was thus interrupted it becomes probable that Æthelwold did not retain possession of the estate of Abingdon. Piecemeal, the lands within the hundred were given to the church in succeeding years, and the power of the abbot in the region around this house was definitely consolidated by the rights of jurisdiction given him by Edward the Confessor.[2]

In the previous pages stress has been laid especially upon those details which bring the early monastery of Abingdon into touch with the general condition of the country. It may be well, in conclusion, briefly to review the scattered facts which relate peculiarly to the fortunes of the house, the predecessor of the great abbey of north Berkshire in the Middle Ages. By a credible tradition, recorded as early as the tenth century, the monastery was founded in the seventh century. It came into being, as its story was told in the Norman period, through a grant of lands by a West Saxon underking named Cissa to his kinsman Hæha. Although unsupported by contemporary evidence, the tradition of the later abbey may fairly be accepted in regard to the manner of its origin : a fragmentary charter of probable authenticity shows Hæha associated with a lady named Ceolswyth as the

[1] A. C. ii. 258.
[2] C.D. 840. Apparently the meeting-place of this hundred lay somewhere near Dry Sandford, A. C. ii **114**, ' Haec, autem ecclesia unum hundred in Samford [Claud. C ix, Sandford] . . . continet.' The context shows that this passage refers to Hormer hundred.

recipient of lands from King Ini near the beginning of the eighth
century. Before the year 709, Hæha had become the abbot of
the house of Abingdon, a little monastery of twelve monks.
Standing in the debatable valley of the middle Thames, the
church passed alternately under the protection of the kings
of Wessex and of Mercia : memories of the political vicissitudes
of the region were still preserved in the abbey in Norman days,
though they were imperfectly understood. When, in the year
779, King Offa of Mercia defeated at Bensington King Cynewulf of Wessex, Berkshire for some seventy years became annexed
to the Mercian kingdom, and the monastery of Abingdon passed
under the rule of the Mercian bishops of Leicester. In 944,
Ceolred, bishop of this see, obtained privileges from King Beorhtwulf of Mercia for certain monasteries in his diocese, of which
Abingdon was one. Nothing definite is recorded concerning the
internal history of the house in this its earliest phase ; and,
according to tradition, its life was interrupted by its destruction
at the hands of the Danes who invaded Wessex in 871. It next
appears in being in the first years of Æthelstan's reign, when, as
' St. Mary's stow in Abingdon ', it received the village of Uffington from the ealdorman of East Anglia. A shadowy abbot, whose
name as recorded in the twelfth century may represent an Old
English Cynenoth, figures as grantee in suspected charters of
King Æthelstan ; he is succeeded as ruler by a certain Godescalc,
a scholar of presumably German origin. All through the reigns
of Æthelstan and Eadmund the king possessed a royal residence
in Abingdon, revealed to us upon the occasion when the former
king treated there for his sister's marriage with the messengers
sent by Hugh, duke of the French. As a little monastery
established upon a royal estate, the house of Abingdon, poor
and ill served, continued until King Eadred, just before his
death, and under the advice of his mother, placed it under
the authority of Æthelwold of Winchester, the commanding
figure in the revival of monasticism in tenth-century England.

With this event begins the unbroken life of the monastery.
Its importance as a school of monks in the tenth century under
Æthelwold, its greatest abbot, has tended to obscure its insignifi-
cance in earlier times. Yet so far as we can see it was only
chance that directed that Abingdon should be the scene of

Æthelwold's labours. In the tenth century there were monasteries in Berkshire at Kintbury[1] and Cholsey[2]; in an earlier age there had been a monastery at Cookham.[3] We have no warrant for the assumption that Abingdon, when Æthelwold received it, differed in any significant way from any of these little houses. The early history of Abingdon is of interest because through its later development some memory has been preserved of the fortunes of one among the many *monasteriola* which studded the shires of Wessex in the eighth and ninth centuries. Some among the early documents of Abingdon were preserved in the scriptorium of the later house; monks in the Norman age were interested in remembering the circumstances of its foundation. That they also applied themselves to the invention of details of which the authentic memory had perished has obscured the true story of the origins of their house. It remains possible to recover a faint outline of the history, and the facts which are thus suggested have their significance in relation to the general condition of the country in the age which lies behind the middle of the tenth century.

[1] C. S. 678.   [2] C. D. 716.   [3] See above, p. 22.

INDEX